From the day Jilly Cooper first burst upon the scene with an article in the *Sunday Times Colour Magazine* she has never looked back (although in this book there is a chance for the reader to do so). Her name is now a household word. She is read and discussed all over the world — her postbag bulges with approving and disapproving letters. She delights some people with her witty comments on day-to-day life, problems and people, and she irritates others beyond belief.

Here is a chance to read again some of her most famous pieces. Whether she is coping with uninvited guests, going hunting, describing her favourite fads and fancies, or merely reporting on the scene around her, her articles are full of laughter laced with good common sense. The ideal Jilly Cooper reader says: 'That's just what I've always been thinking — but I wouldn't have dared to admit it.'

Jolly Superlative
Jilly Cooper

CORGI BOOKS
A DIVISION OF TRANSWORLD PUBLISHERS LTD

To CYRIL and GWEN
with love and gratitude

JOLLY SUPERLATIVE
A CORGI BOOK 0 552 11801 X

Originally published in Great Britain by
Eyre Methuen Ltd.

PRINTING HISTORY
Eyre Methuen edition published 1979
Corgi edition published 1981

This book is set in 10/11 Bodoni

Corgi Books are published by
Transworld Publishers Ltd.,
Century House, 61–63 Uxbridge Road,
Ealing, London, W5 5SA

Made and printed in United States of America
by Arcata Graphics
Buffalo, New York

Introduction

The original edition of this book had a picture of me and my beloved, and late lamented, English Setter on the cover. How the memories come flooding back. He had to be put down because he had a penchant for killing cats. I still miss him to this day. There are two pieces about dogs in this collection of which I am very fond. One of them describes a visit to Crufts which has more recently served me better than I could have imagined at the time, since a children's book I am currently writing is set at a dog show. The other is about the revolt of the Putney Common dog walkers, also coincidentally part of the background to another book I am writing at the moment about life on our beautiful common. To a writer, everything around him is material. So many of the episodes described in this book have furnished me with ideas for future work. I think my favourite pieces in this volume are the description of the visit to the Seven-a-Side tournament at Twickenham and the description of Princess Anne's wedding which got me into so much hot water. There is a sequel to the Seven-a-Side piece which always makes me laugh. I described in writing it how all around me the rugger crowd were gorging themselves on cakes and sandwiches and pies. One man in particular impressed me so much with his appetite that I referred to him as "a piggy". Imagine my surprise when a few months later, watching a Test match at Lords, a large munching figure turned to me and said, "You don't recognise me do you?" To my negative reply he said: "I am the piggy you wrote about at Twickenham."

My thanks are due to the Editor of *The Sunday Times* in which most of these articles first appeared and also to the editors of *Time Off* and *Vogue*.

Contents

My Day

My day begins about eight o'clock when my husband, scented and suited for the office, tells me he's off and will I ring him when I'm conscious. His departure is the cue for anarchy to break out, the dog jumps on to the bed, my son steals down from upstairs bringing stories to be read, and gets into bed too. My daughter, thank God, is confined to her cot, or no doubt she'd be in fighting as well. Groggily I read *Peter Rabbit* and *Tom Kitten*, and my son goes off to get dressed.

I then lie and brood on all the things I didn't do yesterday, principally start a piece for *The Sunday Times* on the subject of Joy which is due in tomorrow.

The dog starts licking my face, which means he wants to go out. I put on my dressing-gown and take him into the garden. The birds are in full flood, the roses brimming with rain from a recent storm. Joy is a summer morning, I decide, groping for a first paragraph.

The dog, perfidious creature, takes advantage of my reverie to escape through a hole in the fence and, dodging the milkman and the postman who make valiant attempts to stop him, is now hell bent for the Common. I chase him, trying to keep my dressing-gown within the bounds of decency. People walking their dogs look at me incredulously. I finally corner the dog in a neighbour's garden, giving heart attacks to two hamsters in a cage.

Back at home, the New Zealand Nanny is giving the children breakfast, and a dreadful mewing cacophony reminds me the cats need feeding. The dog eats his own breakfast and tries to eat the cats' too.

9

My husband rings to say 'Good Morning' and to ask me if I can remember if we're going out this evening, or even worse, if anyone is coming to dinner with us. I fail to provide the information. In a vain attempt to impose some organisation on the household, the Nanny tied an engagement book to the telephone last week, but I have already stolen it to write in.

My husband then says he thinks Joy is a bloody silly subject to write about when I'm so pushed for time, and rings off.

By this time the Irish housekeeper who comes in daily has arrived and been told that the dog has broken the fence down again. Muttering and armed with hammer and nails, she goes off into the garden. My Italian daily, who comes weekly, arrives next and starts on the drawing-room. I collect daily women like other people collect stamps — I'm so touched anyone might want to clean my house, and so terrified of being stranded with no one that at one time I had four working for me.

I then settle down to the greatest intellectual exercise of the day: making a shopping list. How can I possibly get worked up about what I want to eat for dinner at nine o'clock in the morning? Suggestions come from all sides — in New Zealand, Italian and Irish — rather like the League of Nations.

The children go out shopping with the Nanny. Blessed peace invades the house. I settle down to work, and think about Joy. The dog, who is bored, comes in and selects a novel from the bottom row of the shelf and starts chewing it. I remove it, he selects another. I give up.

The telephone goes. Would I like to sit on a panel travelling round the country, answering questions about disposable nappies? Thanks awfully, I say, but no. The telephone rings again. Did I realise that I'd changed the hero's hair from blond to black in the second instalment of my romantic serial for 19 — and did I realise the third instalment was due on Thursday? I didn't. I get moving on Joy.

I type desultorily for a few minutes, and look up Joy in the quote dictionary. God — there are nearly two columns, someone must once have had some bright ideas on the subject.

It is quite hot so I take my typewriter into the garden. The dog buries an old pork chop he has found in the dustbin. The Irish housekeeper has now mended the fence, it looks like some sort of *objet trouvé*: nailed-on orange boxes, prams and the remains of an old typewriter blocking up the holes. The dog inspects it with interest, I suspect he is working on a book on great escapes.

The telephone goes again. Someone reminding me we were supposed to be lunching. I was just about to ring you, I lie, I'm afraid the children have got 'flu.

The doorbell goes, a market research lady with upswept hair wants my view on a new orange drink with egg mixed into it. Unable to resist an ego trip, I ask her in. After all I've got all day to write about Joy.

As she is leaving, the telephone rings yet again. 'Are we meeting at one o'clock or one-fifteen,' says the voice of one much too important to my career to stand up.

'One-fifteen,' I say meekly.

It is now 12.30. Into the bath, switch on the Carmen rollers. The blasted telephone rings yet again, a girlfriend thinks her husband is going off her.

'Everything is getting on top of me these days,' she sobs, 'except Henry.'

I commiserate for ten minutes, by which time the minicab has arrived to take me to lunch, and my hair will have to go uncurled.

The Irish housekeeper, who has a profound contempt for other people's housework, is cleaning the drawing-room the Italian daily already cleaned this morning. The dog, who has an equally profound contempt for *objets trouvés* has bashed down the fence again. We all surge out to the Common, including the minicab driver, and finally corner him under a plane tree.

Arrive at restaurant with a stream of apologies.

'I'm terribly sorry I'm late but . . .'

'You started late,' says my lunch date, who knows me quite well.

11

The wine waiter arrives.

'Oh just some wine,' I say. 'I must work this afternoon.'

'So must I,' says my lunch date, and orders large gin and tonics.

I decide to pick his brains.

'Have you any views on Joy?' I ask.

'Joy who?' he says.

An excellent Dover Sole, a bottle of wine and several brandies later, I am riding home in a taxi, having promised to write a book by Christmas, which I know I'll never complete.

Euphoria floods through my veins. Ideas are suddenly racing through my head. The Serpentine hangs in the golden haze of late summer. I write frenziedly on the back of my cheque book, cleaning tickets and old bills.

In the King's Road, I pass a children's boutique, and feel suddenly guilty about gallivanting, and leaving my motherless darlings at home. I stop the taxi, intending to buy a couple of T-shirts, but come out with half the shop and a bill for £15. Joy is an adorable family of children waiting to welcome you.

Arrive home to find six children having tea. The din is hideous. The dog greets me ecstatically, putting his paws round my neck. I feel guilty about not buying *him* a T-shirt. Decide I am too much in wine to do any work yet, and take him for a walk on the Common.

There has been another shower of rain which brings out the brightness of the wild flowers, the mare's tail glistens pearly like weed at the bottom of the sea. Stop and gossip to an old lady with a mildewed pug. We share the same vet, appropriately known as Doctor Finlay, whose casebook contains half the dogs in Putney.

'The nice thing about Doctor Finlay,' says the old lady, 'is he remembers all the dogs' Christian names.'

I notice the grass has a red haze in the evening sun — we turn for home. My euphoria steadily evaporates as I spend a good half hour catching the dog. He canters round two feet in front of me, grinning like Tommy Brock and whisking out of reach every time I move towards him. My temper in shreds, I finally grab him by the tail under a hawthorn tree.

We go home — not friends. The children are clamouring for attention. I decide to work after supper instead. Gather together my scanty notes on Joy and start cooking. I put onions in the frying pan, and am suddenly struck by a brilliant pun. I must write it down before I forget it. By the time I have found a pencil, the onions have burnt. Decide against frying new onions, and throw in some lamb chops.

I peel some potatoes. They are new, and I know I should scrape them, but it's so much quicker to carve great quarter-inch slices off the sides. In the garden, I discover, someone has weeded away all the mint over the weekend.

Lunchtime euphoria has totally disappeared. My son wants to be read stories, and selects three which will take at least half an hour, beat him down to two, which still take twenty minutes. I find my daughter very pleased with herself, having shredded her nappy all over the floor — she's the one who should go on that panel to talk about disposable nappies.

My husband arrives grumbling about the awfulness of the 22 bus service. We dine in the garden to enjoy the scent of the tobacco plants. Overhead aircraft make any attempt at conversation impossible.

After dinner my husband and I, who are making a desperate attempt to kick the habit of watching television every night, sit in the drawing-room listening rather self-consciously to Mozart. My husband reads a manuscript, I try to decipher all the notes I made on cleaning tickets in the taxi. Alas they turn out to be the usual mawkish drivel one produces after a liquid lunch.

The telephone goes.

'Yes, of course,' I hear my stepdaughter saying, 'come right over.'

It appears my husband's first wife's second husband is about to descend with a crowd of my husband's first wife's children and family. I and my husband who don't possess the *Who's Afraid of Virginia Woolf* type sophistication needed for such an encounter, beat a sneaky retreat to our next door neighbour's and wait until the coast is clear before we return home.

The bath water is cold. My husband was right all along. Joy is a very silly subject to write about. He is asleep when I get into bed. I lie in the dark. What the hell can I write about? What about insomnia? Seemingly brilliant half thoughts start to flicker through my mind. I wish I had a cleaning ticket and a pencil handy — the dog whimpers in his sleep, a child cries fitfully upstairs and is quiet. Insomnia . . . I am so bored by my own meditations that sleep is not long in overtaking me.

To Butlins with 450 Vicars

I have just spent a riotous two days at Butlins, Clacton, where 450 clergymen from the Diocese of Southwark were due for an annual get together. I had wild visions of rural deans on dodgem cars, and being woken at dawn by a loud-speaker screaming 'Christians, Awakey, awakey!'

Even the most charitable of vicars couldn't claim Butlins was beautiful. A prisoner of war camp once, it still has barbed wire on top of the high fences. Neon signs flash everywhere, and in the chalets there is a dreadful penchant for vermilion, salmon pink and a particularly vicious shade of turquoise. The whole place has the neglected air of a long-abandoned Hollywood set.

On arrival you receive your Entertainment Programme full of rules about not eating in the dorm or making a row after hours in case you wake 'sleeping kiddies'. I was relieved to see I'd just missed organised netball.

The atmosphere was less frenetic than expected. No one was blowing squeakers. Ladies with corrugated perms and white cardigans sat about digesting their lunch. Many of them had left off their roll-ons, and their floral shifts were concertina-ing tight round their hips. A few couples necked lethargically on the side of the pool.

Then the clergy started arriving, and the place was suddenly filled with gales of hearty laughter and the padding of sandalled feet. Most of them were in mufti — some very Hooray Henry with suntanned throats, open-necked shirts, and tennis rackets. Others obviously determined to repudiate any suspicion of the fuddy duddy, wore velvet jackets and their hair coaxed forward into little tendrils.

The in-garment, however, seemed to be the home-knitted green pullover with a motif of dropped stitches.

All were very friendly and greeted each other with firm handshakes, and introductions straight out of University Challenge.

'Richard Miller, Good Shepherd, Parsons Green,' 'Charles Hopkins, Jude the Obscure, Letchworth.'

'This Way To The Blue Camp,' said a large notice. It seemed more fitting that the clergy were all housed in Red Camp.

The next moment I saw the familiar face of our lovely local vicar — looking very glamorous in jeans and a flowered shirt. I asked him if it were compulsory to attend the conference.

'It's frowned on not to,' he said. 'The Bishop of Southwark puts out a three-line whip.'

'The only excuse one can plead,' said an elderly vicar dipping a biscuit into his tea, 'is marital trouble. Unfortunately I haven't had a cross word with my wife in years.'

In spite of gentle grumbling, they all looked very carefree at the thought of four days away from the worries of the parish — hims ancient and modern surging up the stairs to Evensong.

The service took place in a hall with murals of Venetian gondoliers, and Mexican ladies lifting their skirts in the cancan. The hymns sounded wonderful, each vicar singing out as if he were the only one keeping a straggling congregation going, and the responses — with everyone knowing them — sounded like a chorus from *Murder in the Cathedral*.

The Bishop of Southwark, Mervyn Stockwood, gave the address. He is a splendidly flamboyant figure with smouldering deep-set eyes, beneath shaggy eyebrows. Urbane, very much the Prince Bishop, there is also a touch of Mother Jaguar graciously waving her tail. His delivery is frankly histrionic, the thunder, the cascade of epithets, the dying fall, the finger waggling heavenwards. Clad almost entirely in episcopal purple shades — aubergine jacket, and socks, brilliant violet tie, and mauve shirt — he really ought to be re-christened 'Mauve-in'. Bishops according to Sydney Smith are supposed to choose their clergy for a 'drooping down deadness of manner', but if the group gathered round his chalet after the service is anything to go by, Mauve-in picks his staff for their glamour and brio.

He sidled round like a chess bishop, filling glasses, stopping to talk for a minute, breaking up groups and re-introducing people.

'I used to be very shy when I started,' he said. 'I lurked outside people's houses, and as soon as I saw they'd gone out, I'd slip a card through their door saying "the vicar called, but you were out".'

'How are you enjoying the conference,' said a rather arch deacon. 'Personally I always feel the clergy are like manure. All right when spread about, but not too good in a heap.'

A diversion was caused by the arrival of a suntanned David Sheppard, Bishop of Woolwich, who is really a beauty, his black hair hardly touched with grey, exuding manliness and modesty like a John Buchan hero. The rather gaudy amethyst flashing on his finger looks out of place beside the severe dark suit and navy blue shirt.

He said that since he became a bishop he found it more difficult to write his *Woman's Own* column, he seemed to have less contact with the people. No, *Woman's Own* hadn't given him a rise when he became a bishop.

Another Stockwood scorcher rolled up, the vicar of St. Peter's, Morden, who has black curls, burning yellow eyes and is the spitting image of Terry Stamp.

'I'm always being asked for his autograph,' he said.

He began swapping telly one-upmanship gossip with other members of the clergy.

'London Weekend rang me on December 22 — we have liturgical dances at my church — they wanted to film them and for us to provide a 200 strong congregation. I told them to take a running jump, I mean Christmas *is* our peak period.'

17

After High Tea, there was a choice of various bars, or 'Shake it' at the Discothèque. A few of the clergy went off to play the fruit machines or make use of the Self Service Gaiety Foyer. The rest returned to the main hall to watch an albino monk giving a demonstration of contemplative prayer by standing on his head.

'Now I'm imitating a bird,' he cried flapping his arms.

The Clergy — impeccably tolerant — watched him with amused interest. Round the hall were stalls for holy books.

In a side room Bishops' robes, richly jewelled and embroidered crimson, scarlet and gold, hung on coat hangers — reminding one of an evening dress rail in the King's Road. I thought once again of Huxley's definition of the church as a vast and elaborate academy of art.

Back in my chalet, I shivered before the bleakness of snowcemmed walls and overhead lights; it was only when I got into my bath I realised there were no soap or towels. I dried myself on the bathmat, planning a novel called *How Grim Was My Chalet*.

Next day, the rising sun touched the drying underwear of the fat ladies which hung outside their chalets, as a communion hymn rose triumphant from the hall like some pagan chant to celebrate the arrival of morn. Inside the hall David Sheppard was giving a straight bat address full of trendy references to *Godspell*, and the self-interest of the older generation. In front of me a row of large lady deacons with cropped hair gazed at him in wonder.

I always feel the clergy should be protected. As they surged into the Butlins newsagents to buy their morning papers I wanted to fling my coat over the filthy postcards, like Sir Walter Raleigh. Whenever I talked to them I kept saying something unsuitable, then 'Oh God! I'm sorry', and then, 'Oh God I'm sorry for saying "Oh God".'

'Do girls look at you differently when you've got a dog collar on?' I asked a handsome canon.

'A dog collar seems to say "Keep off",' he said. 'People look at you with pity, as though you were a lion at the zoo.'

'I think the dog collar gives one the ring of confidence,' said a little curate primly.

Back for yet another sermon, I was beginning to wilt. This time it was Hugh Montefiore, Bishop of Kingston, suave and elegant in lavender flares and a striped shirt. Unusually tall, very donnish, he has one of those frightfully frightfully voices with an almost Larry the L-a-amb pronunciation of the 'A's.

His sermon was a dazzling affair about the kingdom of heaven, which must have provided the listening clergy with sermon fodder for months. Stockwood and Sheppard watched him with enigmatic expressions on their faces. Were they impressed, I wondered, or irritated because he was so brilliant, or just wondering what was for lunch?

Later as I sat in the Blinking Owl Bar, downing gins and tonics, listening to a group discussing the Holy Spirit in tones of passionate seriousness, I felt I had slipped back five centuries to some ecclesiastical hairsplitting before the dissolution of the monasteries.

Up in the Viennese Ballroom, Bishop Hugh, who'd just told us it is not the duty of the church to pass judgement, was busy judging a Miss She Competition. Apart from the asinine comments of the compère, and the plastic vine on the ceiling, and the Redcoats in their groin-level minis, he might have been officiating at some society wedding, for all the competitors were rigged out amazingly in huge picture hats, long white gloves and best dresses.

'They're all pros,' whispered one of the Redcoats. 'They book in for three days just for the beauty contests.'

'Now ladies,' the compère jollied the audience, 'watch out for the She Mystery Man who may be among you.'

'We've got a camp padre here you know,' said the Redcoat.

Afterwards the Bishop and I wandered round the camp, passing clergymen playing vigorous games of tennis.

'Funny how you can tell the clergy from the Butlinites,' he said, 'they look more purposeful somehow.'

A man and a small child were roller skating across the

skating rink, the man going backwards, holding out his hands to encourage the child, not touching her but there if she should stumble.

'There you have a perfect modern parable of God and one of his flock,' said the Bishop.

In the swimming pool, the lady deacons were totally immersed in a game of water polo.

It was time to go.

As I sadly waited for a taxi to take me to the station, I had a last chat with one of the male Redcoats.

'We like having the clergy,' he said, 'they're so well behaved and nicely spoken. The Archbishop came last year, we all loved him, he used to get bored of all those dreary sermons and wander off into the discotheques and really talk to the people. His favourite record was "Jesus Christ Super Star".'

'The best vicars' shindig I ever saw,' he went on lowering his voice, 'was in Bangor, when they coincided with the Cartoonists of Great Britain. They had a cricket match — and the Clergy wiped the board. The cartoonists said it was unfair — the clergy being so used to keeping their hands in a praying position, they never dropped catches.'

Sold to the blonde . . .

Crossing the threshold of Sotheby's you feel the sacred frisson, that special reverence evoked by great art and vast sums of money.

Polite young men directed me through warehouses crammed with headless statues to a sale of 'rare wines'. It was like being in church. Everyone whispered except the auctioneer, who addressed us in bell-like tones from a pulpit. Handsome, drawn-faced, he had the grave courtesy of Plantagenet Palliser. On closer inspection he turned out to be an old flame of my sister-in-law. I resisted winking at him in case he thought I was bidding.

'Here is a nice case of Moet et Chandon for your inexpensive birthday party,' he said with a slight smile.

The audience shook with silent laughter, as the lot went for £68. No one says 'going going gorn' any more apparently, because it takes up too much time. A jeroboam of Château Mouton Rothschild went for £230, a dozen bottles of Château Lafite for £250 — rather like that scent at nine guineas an ounce that used to flavour pink Camay.

A man on crutches came in with a pretty girl holding a baby who started bellowing and was promptly removed. Like me, it was probably desperate for a drink.

Unable to stand any more talk about champagne, I moved over to a sale of Old Masters. The room was packed, the crowd really smelling of money: the women suntanned, many of them chewing gum, wore those pale silk jersey dresses that cost such a fortune in dry cleaning bills.

The auctioneer, a patrician Cyril Fletcher, had come-to-bid eyes and a spotted tie.

21

'Who's he?' I asked.

'The Chairman of Sotheby's,' whispered my neighbour. I felt slightly shocked — as though I'd gone into Marks and Spencers, and Mr Marks himself had risen from behind a counter and measured me for a bra. On the left were a chorus of aesthetes in coloured shirts and wide knotted ties, like a Harvey and Hudson window.

Bidding was brisk, a Crivelli madonna and a Jan Van Heem still life going for vast sums. I can take or leave rare wines, but I really coveted some of those pictures. I felt a sudden longing to escape from the venal world of Bond Street into one of those shining untroubled seventeenth century landscapes and sleep on the grass or paddle knee deep with the cows in one of those misty reedstrewn rivers.

Then an El Greco Christ came up for sale, and the atmosphere in the room changed electrically, eyes swivelling left to right, watching the chief bidders like a Wimbledon crowd.

Equally athletic were the eyebrows of the auctioneer recording bids, as they rose from £40,000 to £50,000. Was the huddled figure on the right going any higher? He shook his head. Everyone turned round trying to read the thoughts of the dispassionate ageless man on the left. His companion whispered to him, he nodded, the bidding rose to £51,000. There was a pause. The auctioneer looked round with polite incredulity. Was no one going any higher? Down came the gavel.

On to Sotheby's Belgravia to a sale of nineteenth-twentieth-century collector's items — all those lovely nostalgic toys like Bagatelle and Diabolo that one's grandmother used to unearth when one went to stay as a child.

The atmosphere here was much jollier than Bond Street, men in maroon overalls carting goods back and forth, surreptitiously playing with the toys as they waited. Suddenly a monkey bandsman would break into a frenzied tattoo, or a musical box open and a burst of tinkling notes come out.

A wooden ark went for £35, a clockwork mouse orchestra for £70.

I was dying to buy a clockwork goat with real fur which

leapt from the ground. But I was too timid to start bidding, and it went unsold. A beautiful music box went for a considerable sum. Two assistants stepped forward to remove it, then both stepped back, thinking the other had hold of it. The box crashed to the floor, rosewood splintering, entrails and machinery spilling out. 'Sale cancelled', sighed the auctioneer.

I was still kicking myself for not buying that goat when two men staggered on carrying a vast early twentieth-century carrier's sign of four horses pulling a wagon under a turquoise sky. 'Brighton and Maidstone' said the inscription on the picture.

It was too much of a coincidence. Maidstone is the name of our ludicrously doted-upon English setter, and I knew that regardless of size and price I had to have that painting.

Someone kicked off at £5. Rapidly the bidding rose to £12. Gingerly, I raised my hand. The auctioneer looked in my direction. Funking it, I hastily pretended to be brushing back my hair. An old biddy offered £15 and, determined not to be outbiddied, I caught the auctioneer's eye and nodded.

'£18 — I'm bid.'

Then like a swimmer who plunges into an icy river and suddenly discovers he can crawl, I was off, bidding away like a maniac, winking, blinking, and nodding. A terrible God-like feeling assailed me.

Unconcerned I bid away the housekeeping money, then the paper bill. Away went the Nanny's salary, and the money for my daughter's new shoes. The other bidders fell by the wayside. Only a girl in a peasant blouse with ebony curls was still in the race.

She raised the bid. I raised it. She raised it to a ludicrous sum.

None of us would eat for a week. Even the dog would have to survive on art alone, but the latent Guggenheim was unleashed in me. I made a higher bid, and waited, heart thumping.

It seemed an eternity. Then the black curls shook in defeat. Down came the gavel.

'Sold to the blonde,' said the auctioneer.

I was swinging from the chandeliers, felt as though I'd won the pools. That I was paying out a fortune rather than receiving one seemed quite irrelevant. Brighton and Maidstone was mine.

I looked across at the girl with black curls. Her shoulders slumped in disappointment and suddenly I felt terribly mean. Perhaps she had a dog at home called Brighton.

Grave concerns

One of my favourite pastimes, being a compulsive reader, is wandering through cemeteries and deciphering the inscriptions on the tombstones. Some are so poignant:

Thirty years I was a maid
Thirteen months a wife
Thirty hours a mother
And then I lost my life.

Others are just hilarious:

The Giver of Life knocked at the door
Our Phyllis went to answer.
(Bloody Fool).

Each tells its own story. I long to know what happened to Maud Lampson, lying in Brompton Cemetery: 'Misunderstood in life, peaceful in death, beloved wife of Sir Curtis Lampson' and what on earth was George Standish up to when he 'died suddenly in Paris in April 1899 at the age of 58'?

I love the flowery language, too. 'A happy release' — which sounds like an optimistic PR handout — or 'Joy cometh in the morning', like a laxative ad.

In one corner lies 'dearest Adelaide, beautiful, gifted and resting' — like most of the actresses one knows: in another, one of those strawberry roan marble horrors has been erected in devoted memory of 'Mum, have a good sleep, dear.' How Mum can possibly sleep with Chelsea Football Ground next door is beyond comprehension.

Another of my favourite haunts is Putney Cemetery. 'No Parking,' says an optimistic sign outside. Wild lavender and brambles swarm over the graves. Unused to visitors the pigeons only clatter into the yews when you're practically treading on their tails. A friendly ginger Tom escorts you round, rolling over on the graves — a kind of Requies-Cat.

But do the dead really rest in peace? At the bottom of the cemetery lies Charles Seton, who had the temerity to bury himself in the same grave as both his first and second wives. Their tombstone lurches drunkenly at 650 as though displaced by frenzied roughhousing underneath.

A few yards away stands a large stone, sacred to the memory of Sarah Jane, died 1885, 'faithful servant for 42 years of the Hervey family.' Nice to know *some* people could keep a Nanny in those days.

People are so charitable about the Dear Departed too. They always forget how he left the top off the toothpaste, or forgot to clean the bath.

I love all the exotic names. John Ball Ball, 'beloved of his many children,' Elphinstone Pourtales, Augustus Horsfall, Abraham Lincoln Moore, second son of George Washington Moore (I bet he got teased at school).

What is horrifyingly rammed home is the infant mortality of the nineteenth century. Tears sting the eyes for Albert and Emma, twins aged three, and little Annie Davenport, aged two days, and the 'three beloved children of the Rev and Mrs McConnell, who were cut off by fever in the short space of thirteen days to the inexplicable grief of their parents.'

In Barnes Old Cemetery, one often finds little children buried in the same vault as their parents or ageing grandparents — which seems more humane somehow than Brompton Cemetery's tendency to place all the children in the same 100 yards of grass: so you find 'our poppet Carole Anne, aged 2 months', 'Vanessa aged three', and rows and rows of tiny urns for Joyce and Timmy and Doreen, stretching out with all the heartrending desolation of a children's ward.

What staggers me as a twentieth century agnostic is the stoicism with which the Victorians accepted having whole families snatched away from them. Take Arthur Marshall. 'Daddy's Boy died aged 6 months.'

'God lent this little lamb on earth
To cheer us for a while.
Then Christ the Shepherd gathered him
He left us with a smile.'

Or Mabel and Kessie, aged four and nine months, who 'are now with Christ, which is far better.'

How did they know it was far better? One wants to crash one's hand down on a table and shout, how could they be sure? — particularly at a time of year like this when the sun broods on the lichened stone, the horse chestnut stretches out its pale green parachutes, and spring rampages across the Common making it a joy to be alive.

Occasionally one is glad to find a sense of outrage breaking through the stoicism. On the tombstone of a young wife, who died aged 22, her husband had written: 'To my sweet Alice, her life was craved, but God denied. Thy will, not mine, be done.'

But on the whole cemeteries are happy places. Have you noticed how sweetly the birds sing in them? Going through Barnes Old Cemetery every morning with all the blackbirds and thrushes in full flood is like entering the orchestra pit. I like to think they're singing to cheer up the dead, but my husband says it's because they're pleased about finding the fattest worms.

And now the season of 'sleeping out' has begun, the cemetery is even more inhabited. Visiting tramps stretch out on the vaults at night, and the other morning I found my fellow dog walkers clicking their tongues over a splendid orgy which had occurred the night before. A copy of *The Sunday Times* was spread out under a great Spanish oak as bedding, and on a nearby grave stood two chewed raw onions, a ball of yellow wool, an empty bottle of VP sweet wine — and a suspender belt.

Rather like Thurber's Nat Bruge, who watched 'the moon coming up lazily out of the old cemetery in which nine of his daughters were lying. And only two of them were dead.'

I'm sure the dead like to be remembered. One notices sadly the blaze of spring flowers on a new 1974 grave when nearby lie neglected graves of people only buried in the Sixties. In Putney Cemetery, overgrown with ivy and strewn with conker husks, lies the tomb of Ethel Wilkes who died one hundred years ago. 'Weep not my children,' says her epitaph, 'I am not dead but sleeping.'

Today no one weeps for her. The yew trees curl their long roots round her dreamless head, and the brambles catch at one's coat as one leaves. Stay oh stay, forget not yet, they seem to plead. Sad that however much people loved you in life you are soon forgotten unless you produce some work of immortality: one remembers Cocteau visiting Proust's deathbed, and observing the 20 manuscript volumes of *A la Recherche* on the mantelpiece, 'continuing to live like the ticking watch on the wrist of a dead soldier.'

As you get older, I suppose, you get more possessed with death. In your twenties you read the engagements and marriage columns, then you marry and concentrate on the births. Soon I'll be scanning the death columns.

It reminds me of that sad old *Punch* joke. 'Nearly all our best men are dead — Carlyle, Tennyson, Browning, George Eliot. And I'm really not feeling very well myself.'

At Lords

Now that the captains and wicketkeepers have departed, and the battle's tumult has moved to White Hart Lane, now that the bells have tolled the knell of parting Ray . . . I would like to tell you of two days I spent at the Lord's Test last week.

The first thing I noticed on arrival at the ground was a large stand saying Rovers Only. I imagined a great crowd of dogs inside, all barking, slobbering over one another and generally creating chaos.

The second thing that struck me was hordes of glamorous men looking all beamish and excited to be there, clutching *The Times* and their first surreptitious glass of beer. *Quelle richesse*, I thought — but I was wrong. Men watching cricket aren't interested in girls. There is something about going through a turnstile that seems to de-sex the male, a kind of symbolic emasculation.

The Lord's Test is in fact a great misogynists' jamboree, where men revert to their schooldays when girls were soppy dates. Wandering round on my own, I felt as though I'd strayed into the Athenaeum or a Gents.

Lord's is also a piggies' High Noon. Fellow spectators never stopped eating and drinking. All round me, they rushed back and forth slopping four pints of beer at a time, smacking their lips as they unpacked vast hampers, choking on scotch eggs, guzzling and swilling and stuffing themselves with pork pies, cream cakes and buns.

'Being out of doors makes one so hungry,' said a fat girl as she embarked on her fifth cheese roll.

I was also disturbed catching glimpses of long golden

manes trailing down bare suntanned backs and thinking Yow! Naked girls! What is Lord's coming to? Then the back would turn round and I'd be confronted with a beard or a large hairy arm reaching for the Party Seven.

On my left was an eager pink-faced girl and her fiancé who was wearing a Free Forester tie. He was initiating her into the mysteries of the game.

'Well, first that chap bowls six balls, then another chap bowls six.'

'Why six?' she said fondly.

'Well, six is a useful sort of number,' he said patiently.

'Get out while you can,' I wanted to shout at her, 'you don't know the hours of spreading sandwiches and getting grass stains off flannels that await you.'

There was so much going on off the field, that one was almost able to forget the cricket. I tried to watch, but it was very dull. The West Indies scored 87, when England got a second wicket, and everyone perked up, like that moment in a pub when you've all been clutching empty glasses for ages, and someone suddenly offers to buy a round of drinks.

Lunch — and the piggies all trotted off to buy more food. While queuing half an hour for a sandwich I marvelled at the élan of the West Indians as they paraded up and down, so tall and princely with their flashing jewellery and their coloured suits — turning Lord's into a male Ascot.

Lunch over, Kanhai batted on and on — from a distance he seemed only a little old man with grey hair. The piggies were still guzzling; the choc bar consumption had reached pyrotechnic heights, and the beer intake was hotting up too — almost a can a minute. Illingworth came on to bowl.

The pink-faced girl was now wilting in the face of a barrage of information from her fiancé:

'Now that was an off break. Watch carefully, he may do it again.'

'Why are they clapping now?'

'Because he's putting his sweater on.'

30

The poor girl looked utterly bemused.

'What do you think of the game?' asked her fiancé.

'Oh lovely,' she said faintly.

'But they're such a long way away. I can't see their faces.'

'Watch their feet, that's far more interesting.'

In fact the part of the players' anatomy one is most conscious of is their bottoms, whether they're running up to bowl, bending in the slips, or standing with their backs to you in the deep. I kept myself awake deciding which player had the most boring bottom. In the end Underwood and Arnold tied for first place.

Kanhai got his hundred, the West Indians exploded in jubilation. T-shirts were covered in beer stains, children balanced along the boundary rails.

I spent hours tracking down a loo. Lord's typically was swarming with Gents, but not with Ladies. Once there, I heard a great roar of applause, a wicket had fallen. It's just as my husband says, you only have to go for a pee and something exciting happens, so you have to rush back zipping up your trousers to find you've missed a hat trick. I was told the illustrious Warner Stand has slits cut in the loo walls so you needn't miss a ball.

Boycott was fielding nearby, and his fan club much in evidence, cheering him every time he put a finger to the ball. What a strange tense creature he is, with his collar turned up against some imagined storm, his sleeves rolled down and left unbuttoned, and his cap with the long beak-like peak like Ducky Daddles in my son's Henny Penny story.

On the second day, as West Indian spirits soared, the English crowd seemed to surrender and abandon themselves to the sheer voluptuous pleasure of watching great cricket. It was as though Sobers and Julien had assumed a divinity, and we were witnessing not just a contest between England and the West Indies, but between men and gods.

Halfway through the morning Fletcher dropped a catch, and suddenly the whole ground was hissing with speculation as though onions had been tossed into a pan of boiling fat. The Boycott Fan Club grew more and more clamorous.

'Put Boycott on to bowl.'

'Come on Sir Geoff-free, when's the Queen goin' to recognise you?'

Boycott gave them a pussycat smirk.

Fifties came and went. Poor bowlers — all that pounding and windmilling to no avail. Poor Illingworth seemed to have aged ten years in two days.

In front of me a piggy ate a whole ginger cake and then a Swiss roll, straight down, peeling off the paper like a choc bar but in an abstracted way as though he was only eating to stem his misery. I didn't blame him. I've always thought the only thing that makes cricket bearable is to be backing the winning side.

But suddenly there was a bonus. Greig was sent to field in the deep, just in front of me, and goodness what a beauty he is, tall and golden as a sunflower, with massive shoulders and long legs! Cricket has found an answer to David Duckham at last. And I wouldn't mind making Hayes while the sun shines either.

Greig returned to the boundary to consistent barracking. He mis-fielded a ball.

'The summer's running out for you, Phyllis,' shouted a wag.

'Why are they all so vile to him?' I asked.

'He's too good looking and too useless to have crowd appeal,' said my neighbour. 'Oh shot, sir, shot, what a lovely shot!'

Finally Kanhai put England out of their misery and declared. England came out to bat, and calypso was followed by collapso, to the extremely irritating ecstasy of the West Indians. The Battle of Kanhai had become a slaughter.

As I was leaving, I bumped into the pink-faced girl and her Free Foresters fiancé. She looked as if she were sleepwalking.

'Don't worry,' he was saying briskly, 'you'll get the hang of it by the fifth day.'

What makes Sir smile

A subject I constantly ponder on is whether there is a lot of adultery about or not. My mini-cab drivers, who are the fountain of all wisdom, claim that it has reached epidemic proportions in Putney.

'I mean, a bloke sees his mate have a bit on the side, Jilly, and he wants some too, don't-'ee?'

Certainly every day I walk my dog on the common I see couples parked on what is known locally as the Eternal Triangle, a piece of land flanked on one side by the tennis courts, on the other by the graveyards, with an avenue of chestnuts on the hypotenuse.

There they sit in their cars, chain-smoking, arms along the back of the seat, misting up the windows, discussing perhaps whether he should leave Norma or whether the office crone has rumbled them; gazing unseeingly at the lichened tombstones, reminders of man's fleeting mortality.

I myself suspect that adultery is on the increase because in the past fortnight three friends I haven't seen in months have suddenly summoned me to expensive lunches and greeted me with a feverish glitter in the eye. Then it all comes spilling out:

'Do you remember that rather quiet vet who fixed Wellington's paw at Christmas . . . ?'

There must also be numerous liaisons seething below the surface like vice-bergs that one never knows about. For as Shakespeare said:

'Many a man there is . . . holds his wife by th'arm

That little thinks she has been sluiced in his absence
And his pond fished by his next neighbour, by
Sir Smile, his neighbour.'

Masterly that Sir Smile — a sort of wolf in sheet's cloth-
ing — and I bet numerous Sir Smiles are cleaning up in the
country round those cottages where the husbands abandon
their wives during the week, while they're off typist-
hunting in London.

There is possibly a lot of adultery at the moment —
because people are on edge and uncertain of the future, and
inclined to snatch at happiness, however ephemeral. Inflation doesn't help either. There is a feeling everywhere that
you may as well eat, drink and make Mary, because
tomorrow you won't be able to afford her.

There's no doubt that adultery is very expensive — not
the act itself but, rather like curry, it's the side dishes that
set you back; all those presents and wooing lunches and
taxis across London to spend two minutes at a party to
establish an alibi. Then there are the hotel bedrooms (even
for two hours you have to pay for the whole night — in
American motels it's known as the hot-sheet trade) and the
bunches of flowers afterwards for the wife because you feel
so guilty.

'Do not adultery commit. Advantage rarely comes of it.'
Clough wrote that but it's not entirely true. It doesn't
always end in tears — usually in pied-à-terres. Admittedly, if you've got a happy marriage, adulterous intent
must be construed as greed rather than hunger. But my
husband says even though one likes home cooking best, one
yearns to eat out in restaurants from time to time.

And looking at those couples huddled together on the
Triangle I can't help thinking that adultery is sometimes
the only shaft of sunlight that makes an utterly drab life
bearable.

One woman writing to the *Daily Mail* recently said she'd
been absolutely beastly to her husband since she decided to
give up her lover: and 99 per cent of her women friends,
she added, would like to have an affair (alas names and

addresses not supplied).

Why do they want to? Because 'we love being in love and that's the truth on't.' And few things equal the early stages, tearing home late but so flooded with euphoria that you don't mind if the children splash you in the bath or the dog has chewed the head off your fox fur. Your looks improve dramatically, your husband starts fancying you twice as much, everyone flourishes.

Then things start going wrong and everyone cops it. You start snapping at the children as you feverishly count the toys scattered on the nursery floor (if it's an odd number, he still loves me), getting more and more depressed like Mariana of the Moated Grange as night approaches, knowing he won't ring after 5.30 because it's not safe.

Try to get over him my dear, say the women's magazines, as though he were the horse in gym.

Sometimes if the husband finds out, it helps the marriage. Having neglected his wife shamefully he suddenly becomes wildly attentive, like the English raising hell when they learn that some Old Master they've never bothered to look at is about to be sold to the Americans.

But on the whole the important thing is not to get found out. My husband may be pleasuring half London but at least he has the good manners not to let me know.

Where do people find the time for a full-scale affair? I suppose it's easier if you haven't got a job. All play and no work make Jack adulterous, presumably.

I am reminded too, of one silly woman who wrote to the papers recently asking: 'What on earth do wives who stay at home all day find to do with themselves?'

'Well,' wrote back one housewife tartly, 'while working wives are at the office, I generally have the pleasure of their husbands.' A telling blow for Women's Libido.

I couldn't stand the strain of living a double life, I'd permanently forget what lie I'd told to whom last week, and it's so easy to come unstuck. 'Thank you very much for putting Michael up so often this summer,' brayed a tweedy country wife striding up to me in Oxford Street.

My jaw dropped. Michael hasn't been near us in years.

If you're caught out the only answer is to lie like hell. One wife going through her husband's suits chanced upon a receipt for dinner and a night for two at the Metropole, Brighton, including several bottles of champagne, and asked him what he'd been up to.

Calmly he studied the receipt. 'It must be my partner's,' he said. 'The rotten sod always uses my name when he gets up to tricks.' And his wife believed him.

As I write this my husband is out at a regimental dinner. Should I start worrying if he returns home entirely sober? In the past when he's gone abroad, I have even put one of the children's chiming Rupert Bear toothbrushes in his sponge bag instead of his own to remind him night and morn of his domestic commitments.

Once you really suspect, of course, nightmare takes over. It's a succession of rifled wallets, steamed-open letters and thinking every wrong number at the weekend is the girl-friend clocking in.

It's odd too how some of the Other Women behave. When one husband I know refused to see his girlfriend any more, she promptly rang up the wife and (most heinous of crimes) spilt the beans. And, not content with that, she went on to kidnap first the wife's dog and then all her dustbins.

Perhaps she was a refusal collector.

Facing up to the music

Being an intellectual snob, I've always slightly disapproved of Promenaders. I know it's 'nice' that keen young music lovers should be able to enjoy concerts at 25p a throw. But they seem to make such a fetish of enthusiasm, and I suspect that if our cat came on to the rostrum in his black tie, and walked up and down the keys, he'd get the usual thunderous applause.

But it was only when I went and promenaded myself last week and met some of the regulars that I realised that Promenaders were a race apart, aficionados, as dedicated as any Chelsea Soccer supporters.

Most of them were bouncy young men with pink faces and puffed-out cheeks who all seemed to be dressed in browns and greens. Friendly, uppity, full of pranks and a sense of their own importance, they swarmed round noisily like the Players in *Hamlet*.

What are the activities of a Promenader other than tremendous enthusiasm, I asked.

'Well, we organise shouts,' said one of them. 'Last week for example we watched a woman in the stalls eating her way through a box of chocolates, so we all chorused: "Don't eat any more madam, or you'll be sick".'

'She went very red and choked on a hazelnut cluster,' said another.

'Sometimes we throw paper darts at each other,' said a third, 'or make hyena calls at the Promenaders up in the gallery. Sometimes they make them back at us, and when we're queuing we chase tourists with rolled umbrellas.'

Judging by the longer and longer queues which curl like

a fox fur round the Imperial College, Proms are becoming increasingly popular, and now, apparently, reach more than 100 million listeners on Radio Three and other channels.

'We're certainly attracting more trendies,' said a very un-trendy Promenader hitching up his baggy trousers. 'Young people like the casual atmosphere. One statement I would like to make,' he went on, 'is that Promenaders do not go into holes in winter. They go to the Festival Hall.'

This was greeted with much hearty laughter.

A young man with a straggly beard said he had been coming to the Proms for nine years, and he had always slept out when queuing for the 'Last Night'.

'That was when I first discovered the streets of London were paved with paving stones,' he said.

More laughter.

I'd forgotten the young could be hearty like this — the only ones I meet are too busy keeping their cool and their hip measurements slinky to be enthusiastic about anything.

In the foyer someone had biroed in the whites of Sir Henry Wood's eyes.

We went down a narrow passage leading to the Arena.

'This is the way the Promenaders run to get the best places up at the front,' said a plump youth. 'You're not counted a proper Promenader until you've twisted your ankle in the rush. Unsuspecting foreign orchestras tuning their violins in the passages are often knocked sideways in the stampede.'

Out in the Arena the familiar fountain played on water lilies and coloured bullrushes, as a spotlight above switched from red to blue to green.

'Someone once put dry ice in the fountain, and it bubbled all the way through Mahler's Fifth,' I was told.

'No they didn't,' said someone else. 'They put Teepol in during the Boulez.'

The Arena was already filling up, mostly young men with beards and their girlfriends, bright-eyed and rosy-cheeked like younger sisters in Chekhov . . . . There was a sprinkling of little nurses in lace-up shoes, carrying coats in case it was cold on the way home. People were sitting on the floor eating grapes and cheese rolls, and passing round beer cans.

Who were the most popular composers now? I asked.

'Well, Handel and Bach are coming back with a vengeance — you'd never have filled the hall with *Solomon* a few years back. And it's very much Mahler, Britten and Walton.'

'Tippet's coming through,' added a pale girl, sounding just like Beatrix Potter.

'We must organise a shout,' said one of the men with puffed-out cheeks.

'There are a lot of men in DJs over there,' said another. 'What about "I can see you Howard Hughes" or "More sex than violence in the Boxes"!'

'We did those last week,' said an earnest girl in a blue smock. Then: 'O look,' she added in ecstasy.

A solitary paper dart drifted down from the gallery.

Suddenly she stiffened. I followed her gaze. Two rather untidy, mild-looking, elderly women, their grey hair turning green in the light, had joined the Promenaders.

'I must summon the OBOES,' said the girl in the blue smock. 'It stands for Old Bags Observation and Evaluation Society,' she added disapprovingly. 'They shouldn't be down here. The older generation simply does not fit in.'

A hyena yell floated mournfully down from the gallery. The Promenaders in the Arena howled back. Another paper dart arrived, and was greeted with loud cheers.

A few debs in Laura Ashley dresses and their escorts joined the ranks, obviously slumming.

'Such fun to go to a Prom,' said one.

The regulars looked at her stonily.

On came the English Chamber Orchestra looking very young and glamorous followed by the conductor — dark and thickset like a suave bearcub. It was his first Prom appearance and, as a change from the standard black, he was wearing a slate-blue velvet suit with braiding and a white frilly shirt.

'Liberace,' yelled the Promenaders approvingly.

His baton was raised. The high jinks were over and the Promenaders settled down to the 'very serious' business of listening to music. Some leant their heads on their hands as if totally exhausted, others hid their faces behind their fingers, eyes closed as if they were in a trance. Others gazed into space, assuming that soppy expression spinsters have when they come down the aisle after taking communion.

It was certainly a familiar programme. A Handel Concerto Grosso, Stravinsky's Pulcinella, the Mozart Clarinet Concerto, and Beethoven's Second. The orchestra was superb, the conductor so vigorous that every hair of his glossy black head was soon drenched with sweat. But I've always wondered how important conductors are. My husband, who used to play in an orchestra, said that he was always trying so hard to read the music, that he never noticed the conductor at all.

It got hotter and hotter. A pretty girl in a broderie anglaise mini blew her nose in the middle of a quiet passage of the Stravinsky. Her boyfriend kicked her in horror. Another girl, fingers over her eyes, was surreptitiously reading the ads in the programme. *Her* boyfriend, who was sitting down, gazed up the pretty girl's broderie anglaise skirt.

I found myself musing on the beautiful cut of the conductor's suit. Really I mustn't be such a Philistine! I put a more ardent expression on my face, and tried to concentrate on the music.

All the same, my feet were absolutely killing me, I was pouring with sweat, and I came to the shaming conclusion that the best way to enjoy Mozart is on the sofa at home armed with a gin and tonic.

The concerto was drawing to its close. One could feel the Promenaders gathering themselves like a great animal to spring into a roar of applause. And they certainly did clap, none of this banging the insides of the wrists together while clutching a satin bag, that one gets with theatre audiences.

In the second half I went upstairs to the Promenaders' Gallery for the Beethoven Second.

'They really get turned on in the dark up there,' said the BBC Press officer. 'Play something romantic like Tchaikovsky and they'll all lie down and neck.'

The atmosphere upstairs was certainly more *louche* and the people better looking. It was like a Henry Moore painting of the Underground during the Blitz. People sitting about with shut eyes, lying wrapped in blankets or flat out on the floor. A constant stream of people strolled back and forth. And if Beethoven didn't inspire people to neck, several couples were sitting at the back with their arms round each other.

Afterwards we all met in the pub. One of the Promenaders who'd had a few started to lecture me:

'People always get us wrong. We're not indiscriminate in our appreciation. We clap everyone a lot, but if anything's really good, we freak out.'

'Nor,' he went on, 'does anyone understand what it's like to be on the Rail.'

For a minute I thought he'd switched to his commuter problems, then realised he was referring to the bar which divides the Promenaders from the orchestra.

'When you're on the Rail,' he said dreamily, 'you get butterflies in your stomach, you feel you are the conductor and the orchestra, then the music starts, and you feel surrounded by friends, friends on the stage, and your friends, the Promenaders, around you.'

'It's a social event, you see,' said a girl in spectacles earnestly. They all agreed with her.

Here lies Jilly Cooper

I got myself into a muddle recently. A nice eager lady from the BBC rang up and asked me to appear on Woman's Hour. Greatly honoured, I agreed. It was only as she rang off, she added that the programme was being recorded in Birmingham.

This put a different complexion on the matter — to Broadcasting House from Putney takes only half an hour; but a trip to Birmingham means a whole work day lost, not to mention meals and magazines and those two pounds I have always to spend in station chemists whenever I go by train.

So I wrote a polite lying letter saying I was heartbroken, but I'd suddenly discovered I had to be in Bristol that day. Return of post comes a telephone call — saying, that was fine, as I was going to be in Bristol, could I record the programme from the BBC studios there?

It was too shaming. But then my husband says I'm incapable of telling the truth, and that I ought to have a plaque on the front of the house saying, Here Lies Jilly Cooper. I kid myself I'm not deliberately dishonest, just born in Pisces, which means, according to my horoscope book, one lies out of general confusion.

Then I remember the times recently I've rung people pretending I've got 'flu, merely because it's a nice day, and I wanted to sit in the sun rather than go out. Another great excuse is: 'I must have eaten something,' or 'struck down by shellfish.' As soon as someone mentions the word 'gastric' you know they're lying.

Thank God at least for the bath: 'Jilly can't talk now,

she's in the bath' or 'she's bathing the children' (usually at some quite improbable hour like 1.45), or 'Jilly and Leo are in the bath' (implying sexual junketing — on no account to be disturbed. People must think we're the cleanest family in Putney).

With such an example it's hardly surprising my children are raving mythomaniacs: my son blaming the three-day week as the reason he hasn't put his toys away, my daughter having scribbled all over the non-wash wall-paper, blaming it on the dog.

But then I'm not sure a truthful nature equips one for life these days. Good secretaries seem to spend all day lying on behalf of their bosses, and one is constantly being told of bright young things who 'bluffed' their way into a marvellous job, which is merely a euphemism for a pack of lies.

Odd too when one lies so often, how embarrassed one is to be caught out, like a friend of mine who said she couldn't lunch with a man because she was on a diet, then later that day went slap into him in the King's Road just as she was stuffing a large cream bun into her face.

Then there was the memorable occasion when my brother, who had been borrowing my aunt's car, told her he had had the brakes checked but actually forgot to do it. And in horrified amusement, he watched her gathering speed down the main road into the village, finally landing up like Ferdinand the Bull surrounded by Cinerarias in the front window of the local flower shop.

I don't lie about *my* age yet — but I do about the dog's, pretending he's younger than he is to justify such rumbustious behaviour. And although my daughter's three next week, I tell everyone she's two, in the hope that people will say how forward she is. My great friend however, has a daughter, who from her seventeenth birthday has been described as nearly eighteen, so everyone gasps and says: 'You can't possibly have a daughter of eighteen.'

Equally I always tell people we've lived in the house less time than we actually have because I feel guilty we haven't done more to it.

Some people lie about their backgrounds — making

43

them grander than they were — but as they become more successful they tend to be less reticent about their humble origins so that people will be even more impressed by the distance they've climbed.

Liking to appear sensitive, I always pretend I was more unhappy at school than I really was, and I went through a stage of telling people my father was a scientist rather than an engineer because it sounded more boffinish and romantic.

I was always brought up to be truthful. It must be marriage that made a dishonest woman of me.

If we're going out in the evening, and I ring up to find out the time, I always report that it's 10 minutes earlier than it really is, so my husband won't harass me. But then if he rings up, he always says it's 10 minutes later to panic me into getting a move on.

Once people are separated they embark on a new set of lies — trying to convince each other how little the other is living on, sending the children over in clean but heavily-darned clothes, leaving the Bentley round the corner and arriving on foot.

A friend of mine wanted to wear his new suede jacket when he took his girlfriend over to his ex-wife to collect the children, but was nervous his wife would think he was wasting maintenance money on new clothes. So his girl-friend suggested he should say that she bought it for him.

Sure enough the moment they arrived the wife's eyes zoomed in on the new jacket.

'Angela bought it for me,' blurted out the husband, adding hastily, 'it was frightfully cheap.'

People lie about the number of people they've been to bed with, men generally bumping up the number. Women, rather like birds, don't seem able to count beyond three. Women lie about their weight and dyeing their hair. Men lie about the time they spend getting from A to B. If they've been drinking in the pub, they always spend 'hours' stuck in traffic jams getting home.

Recently we were lent a Rolls-Royce, worth £17,000, for

44

the weekend. We drove it up to Yorkshire, where my husband and I both grew up. It would have been so easy to pass it off to all our childhood friends as our own. Instead we found ourselves falling over backwards to tell everyone — even policemen checking tyres — that it had only been lent. I think it was the splendour and true blue nature of the car which brought out the latent George Washington in both of us.

Actually George Washington must have been a pain in the ashlar, if he really couldn't tell a lie. He certainly wouldn't have lasted in politics today.

In fact the official lie has become so commonplace, one hardly notices it: Anthony Eden denying there was collusion between the French and the Israelis over Suez; categorical denials that Pompidou was dying or that the Prime Minister's private secretary was going to be given a seat in the Lords; Buckingham Palace flatly denying there was anything between Princess Anne and Mark Phillips. We seem to be suffering from galloping mendacity.

Romantic novels

Reading a romantic novel is a bit like eating a whole box of chocolates or going to bed with a cad. You can't stop during it — but afterwards you wish you hadn't . . .

I don't read many romances today, but in my courting days if things were going badly, I often used to get four a day out of the library, devouring one after another like an anodyne — take every four hours for the alleviation of heartache.

They got me through a bad patch, which is why I particularly welcome a very funny new book *The Purple Heart-throbs** by Rachel Anderson, which traces the torrid hilarious history of romantic fiction from its beginnings in the 1850s to the present day.

Miss Anderson believes romantic novels fill a need — they certainly fill a lot of bookshelves — more than 25 million new books are sold every year. She also believes that like their readers, romantic novelists write to compensate for a lack of romance.

Elinor Glyn, for example, had a most romantic honeymoon. Her husband hired Brighton Public Baths so he might admire his bride swimming in the nude with her long red hair trailing. After that he seems to have become more interested in shooting pheasants, and it was then that she took up her pen. Ouida, another prolific writer, also had husband trouble and never seemed to get the lovers she wanted. E.M. Hull, author of *The Sheik*, lived an unexciting life, married to a dull pigbreeder called Percy.

* Published by Hodder and Stoughton.

She never set foot in the desert.

The desert in fact is one of the favourite settings for romantic novels, but the authors always cheat. Time and again the heroine sets out alone in the midday sun, is apprehended by some mysterious Arab full of Middle Eastern promise, who whisks her off into the dunes. But after a good deal of Sheik rattle and roll, he invariably turns out to be no Arab:

'No Berber could have that insolent easy square jaw, that blunt straight nose, that quietly humorous mouth above a dogged chin . . . . "He is an Englishman," she thought with a queer mounting excitement.'

As this was written in 1970, there is still obviously some corner of a foreign feel that is for ever England.

Arabs, poor things, never get a look in. It's probably out of revenge for such insults that they're being so jolly rotten about supplying oil to people today.

Another favourite setting for romance is the hospital where the heroes are usually surgeons with steely blue eyes and long sensitive fingers:

'It was obvious he was a surgeon, even at 15 yards, surgeons — those under 40 at least — have a look of immediacy about them.'

Romantic novelists pride themselves on getting the medical details strictly accurate, even down to the kisses:

'It was a long kiss and seemed to be controlled by some kind of rheostat like the 12 position graduation of the dimmer switch in the wards, which brings up the lights from a mere hint to a full blaze . . . and somewhere I could have sworn there was a full orchestra playing Ravel's Bolero.'

You go to the operating theatre, it seems, to be entertained — though nobody could accuse this particular novelist of shying away from reality. A few minutes later the heroine tears herself away from the surgeon's clinch, and says brightly:

'I must go, I have to give Mrs Potter a rectal washout.'

As Miss Anderson points out, the charm of romantic novels lies in their preposterousness. Clichés drop like medicinal gum. They never stop smouldering and burning:

47

'Her lips were fire on his cheeks, her arms were chains, chains of fire.'

One is surprised every hero and heroine isn't suffering first degree burns. And they're always raining kisses on one another — presumably to put out the fires — which must be awfully slobbery.

Most writers seem to suffer from adverbal diarrhoea. On a single page, Miss Anderson notes that Diana bursts out passionately, chokes furiously, begins desperately, whereupon he replies drily, goes on evenly, answers carelessly, whispers jerkily, continues sarcastically — to which she understandably murmurs faintly.

Romantic novelists are also raging snobs and much impressed by smart clubs. One hero is Clive Siddeley:

'Before whom all women go down, and for whom little notes are piled high at the Guards Club and the Travellers.'

It is also permissible to go to bed with royalty, but nobody else, and whenever the lower classes appear — which is as seldom as possible — they talk like something out of Benny Hill:

'I like it not,' said the frau, referring to the subject of Gretchen's absence.

'Folly wife, where is your sense?' said Forbach, laughing. 'Mrs Gretchen is as steady as old time.'

Another mania is for Christian names. Oscar and Mona are about to leap off a cliff:

'The time has come, Mona.'

'Yes it has, Oscar.'

'May I kiss you, Mona?'

'Yes, and God bless you for loving me Oscar.'

I presume the whole thing is a conspiracy. If you insert a Christian name every line, it works out at about 6,000 words by the time you've finished the book, which means you do not have to produce so much plot.

I love the titles too: *Love's Surrender* by Maud Driver, or *Under Two Flags* by Ouida, which as the heroine's name is Cigarette really should be re-titled *Under Two Fags*. Then there's *Only a Clod*, about a broad-shouldered valet who makes good — and eventually the heroine.

On the whole, though, every clod does not have a silver lining, for romantic writers just are not interested in the working classes. I remember the editor of a woman's magazine telling me several years ago that fictional heroes must be earning at least £2,000 a year. With inflation they must be on at least £5,000 now.

Heroes are also easily identifiable. They come in two types: Superbore the trustworthy, who has crinkly brown hair and a good-humoured ugly face, and sucks on a revolting pipe, and Superbastard, who is arrogant and domineering, a savage in a Savile Row suit with a hawklike profile. He is a tartar who turns out to have a heart of gold in the last chapter.

Romantic heroines on the other hand are all musical laughs, finely-chiselled noses, delightfully short upper lips and five pairs of knickers. Their hair never gets lank or greasy, they never have spots, their bodies are 'as supple as an arrow ready to fly from Cupid's bow.'

I love their clothes too. They seem to live in feather hats and smart navy outfits.

How do romantic novelists cope with the permissive society? One solution is to seek refuge in the past, or as Barbara Cartland said in a classic line: 'You can write a whole book about someone protecting their virginity, as long as they're in costume.'

But most authors seem to see themselves as today's guardians of morality, the upholders of decent standards — the Festival of Light Fiction.

As an illustration, Miss Anderson takes a Ruby M. Ayres novel published in 1939, but re-issued and up-dated in 1969. In the first edition the heroine wears a hat to lunch, and the hero swears at the waiters: in the 1969 edition, she goes hatless, while he is very polite to the waiters, but, more significant, in 1939 he is up to all sort of tricks 'running his hands over her shoulders and her slim body,' while in 1969, it's all been cleaned up and he doesn't lay a finger on her.

As society gets more permissive, romantic fiction, it seems, gets more straitlaced.

Exchange & Mart

Thank goodness the parcel service is working again. For the past weeks, I have been indulging some of my favourite reading — the pages of postal bargain advertisements in the newspapers.

Now once again for a few strokes of the pen in Kirby Overblow I can become the owner of a saucy sling bra in bombshell black, or an all purpose wonder gadget . . . it digs concrete, fillets sardines, hails taxis, *and* re-upholsters second cousins. At the drop of a postal order, the red G.P.O. van will slow up outside my house bringing an all-in-one corselette in plain wrapper, or an elegant commode stool discreetly disguised as a dressing table.

What a world of opportunity is offered you. You don't keep up with the Joneses in the postal bargain world, you outstrip them. Who could resist the poetry of this wonderful lamp: 'So romantic, so sophisticated, a breathtaking galaxy of light in a myriad of scintillating, iridescent, psychedelic colours, reflected from a host of magic, fibre-like optics, encapsulated in a gorgeous transparent orb. Will draw gasps of admiration from all your friends.'

Then if you've got time for hobbies, there are those kits that are almost impossible to put together: 'Do-it-yourself early gothic antique grandfather clock, as made by Bavarian peasants. Even a child can assemble it' (he'll be a grandfather by the time he's finished!) 'Once this clock decorates your wall you'll receive compliments from relatives and friends.' Could this be a misprint for complaints?

Many of the ads seem to play on people's social insecurity: 'You too can become the life and soul of the party and keep crowded rooms in stitches' with a fun donkey — just pull its ears, and a lighted cigarette shoots out of its bottom. Or there's a bag which laughs maniacally for 30 seconds on the trot — must be a wow at funerals.

Or you can change your life by writing for potted plants: 'Capture the glorious magic of the Swiss Alps with our alpine garden: tiny roses, scented mountain, and true mouth-watering strawberries, which your friends will pop into their mouths when you are not looking' (if they've got a moment between gasping over your transparent orb, or laughing themselves sick over your excreting donkey).

Even more exotic is the: 'Miniature winter flowering garden in a trough. Capture the magic and suspense of the hot sticky crocodile-infested Amazon, right in your own living room. Specially made leakproof trough. Can stand on any piece of furniture.' Even the commode presumably.

They're also very keen on outdoor gardening: potting sheds, greenhouses, even a gardening apron: 'Which has everything except a green thumb. Huge kangaroo pouches free your hands for gardening, not just holding tools.'

I bet the sophisticated young hubby-swapping set in Chipping Sodbury are all writing in for New Mate; three-in-one, the latest eating idea: 'It's a fork, it's a knife, it's a spoon. Ideal for eating spaghetti and gâteau — invaluable for sick.' You jolly well deserve to be sick stuffing gâteau and spaghetti at the same time.

Recently there have been other irresistible novelties: 'Gravestones, free erection England and Wales, or a 12-inch foot comb, 99p. which you manipulate with the toes.'

Then there's Magic Stitch, 'A special needle which sews everything. You can even hem curtains while hanging.' A must for suicides.

The kiddies are not forgotten either, for them there's 'An Accordian, complete in case, with shoulder straps and free tutor.' No wonder there's a teacher shortage.

And just right for the young tycoon is a 'Jumbo-Jet-style briefcase with Jumbo Jet capacity roomy enough for

51

overnight bag (whoever she may be) gusset expands to 7 inches.'

Then we move on to Kinky and Quirky. Ads offering you: 'The most powerful binoculars in the world', or 'telescopes for sport and bird watching', and they always seem to collect the most suggestive adjectives: 'Top quality, low noise, screw mounted, silicone lubricated cassette.'

I adore the drawings too. The people look like characters out of a Peter and Jane story. Huge Junoesque ladies with petal hair and circumflex eyebrows, encased in stretch rubber and whalebone, men smoking pipes in hernia belts, looking like fathers in boys' adventure stories. The wholesomeness and sexless quality seems slightly at variance with the shadiness of the products advertised.

And I like the way the ads hint at foreign manufacture as a selling point: 'Slip Marvel onto your tap, the water is fresh, clear. The rage of health-conscious Scandinavians.' Or there are watches with 'Swiss Movements and virtually unbreakable mainspring.'

Anything slightly risky is described as continental. Which brings us to Duvets. I always muddle them up with bidets, they seem to have the same sophisticated overtones: 'Rip the covers off the seductive bedroom secrets of continental Duvets. No heavy blankets weighing you down, cramping your style. 300 years of continental bedding experience at your finger tips.' Are you ready for that in Leighton Buzzard?

And amid all this steaming sex, there are some pretty bizarre medical ads: 'Give yourself a leg-up, relax with a medically correct, furniture style leg rest' (what the hell's a furniture style leg?). Or there are 'New muscular pain-relieving anklets and wristlets, ideal for outdoor workers, sportsmen and countrymen.' Hard luck Romans and Friends.

The instant-beauty advertisers are out in force too, making ludicrously extravagant claims to 'caress you to an attractive tan in seconds', or 'make you look ten years younger in three minutes' (heaven knows what it does to babies). Then there's 'tooth enamel as used by models', 'combs which curl instantly', 'new De Milo to increase your bustline'. I wonder what it does to your arms.

Everything gets a bit out of hand when they introduce Battery Operated Nailfiles 'for all the family which grooms and files nails in seconds' (a must for aspiring pobbles), and encourages natural growth. On the other hand there's a hair-remover stick 'which discourages natural growth', and yet again 'built-up shoes which encourage growth by making you instantly inches higher.' We'll all be bobbing up and down like Yo-Yos.

One advantage of postal bargains is the anonymity. Lots of people who are shy about buying over the counter must send for bargains such as bedwetting cures, or pull-on hats in lustre deep pile, or pants for the incontinent or hygienic open tights from the continent. Under rainwear, rather bizarrely, they offer 'rubber tunics, aprons, ponchos and directoire knickers to ward off the rain.' Hardly the thing to wear on Putney Common next time I walk the dog in a downpour.

I wonder how many people wear things once and then send them back saying they're not 'absolutely delighted' and they want their money refunded. It would be easy to order a new pull-on felt for church every week, wear it once, and then send it back saying it didn't work. You'd have nothing to lose but your postage.

I wonder too how many Swingers from the Wye Valley are writing in for *Libido*: 'The perfect icebreaker for lively adults. Guaranteed to dispel inhibitions.' Money back if you are not ravished, presumably. Or how many lovely housewives sent up for 'the ideal gift, give your husband 1,000 screws this Xmas.' How the hell did they ever have time to get the turkey cooked?

Finally we move into a *Histoire d'O* and they wear scanty garments with holes in the most extraordinary places. One is constantly being exhorted to 'Write direct for Cat full of delicious intimate fashions.' I bet the poor thing has terrible indigestion.

And they have this obsession with naming everything:

there's 'Marlene, a tantalising boudoir set with saucy fringe trimming', and 'Yolande, a sling bra in sheer nylon' and 'Elena, a devastatingly naughty open fronted negligée and matching pantee set.'

But then they're always naming things on postal bargain pages. In one corner they'll be advertising 'Norman, a genuine fully-lined slipper', in another flogging typewriters called Anita or Gregory.

It must lead to considerable confusion. Imagine some postal bargain lady telling hubby about her day: 'Well, I changed Anita's ribbon, and popped Yolande into the washing machine. Then this afternoon I wrote a rude note to the milkman on Gregory, and when I knew you were coming home I quickly slipped into Marlene and Elena, and wriggled my toes inside Norman.'

Women's mags

I am suffering from a surfeit of lampshades, I am drowning in treacle, I can't wait to run up a stunning jacket in simple garter stitch with useful pockets and an optional belt.

All week I've been reading the latest batch of women's magazines. I don't mean those trendies like *Nova* or *19* but the died-in-the-woollie, crochet-your-own-Royal-Family, gusset-orientated stalwarts: *Woman's Own, Woman, Woman's Realm, Woman & Home, Woman's Weekly* etcetera — all projecting the same cosy insulated world of Women's Glib.

What amazes me is how little their subject-matter has changed over the years. They are still wild about animal stories: cheetahs, donkeys, 'a lovable little scamp of a Siamese kitten', Omar Shariff, even Gillian Fortescue-Edwards, 'expert jockey and riding instructress, who has also shown many a male rally driver her back bumper.'

Doctor, too, is very much in evidence, peddling his bromides:

'I've got terrible cramp in my left leg, Doctor.'

'Don't worry, Mrs L.' I reassured her. 'It will only mean a simple short stay in hospital while they cut your head off.'

'But will I be able to resume normal sexual intercourse afterwards, Doctor?'

'Oh certainly, Mrs L.'

One reader writes in for medical advice: 'My doctor recommended raspberry-flavoured powder for my little girl's thread-worms.' (Lucky little devils.)

While on the subject of worms, one is quite staggered how much tripe the readers go on swallowing about the

Royal Family. One magazine carries an 'important series' on the Queen's wedding:

'The Queen's gown was designed by Norman Hartnell, who was at pains to ensure that the material with which he worked was from silk spun from Nationalistic China silkworms, rather than enemy silkworms from Japan or Italy.'

Another magazine describes the Queen's visit to Swindon, where 'candy-pink screens were erected to conceal unsightly demolition from Royal eyes.'

While yet another had a piece on Prince Edward, which with great perspicacity reveals that 'every month now, the Queen sees that her youngest son is just a little older.'

'Prince Edward,' it goes on, 'looked horrified recently when out on a school walk he saw an old house under demolition.' (Hardly surprising if they're always hidden behind pink screens.)

Every issue is packed with recipes, and pretty revolting some of them are. Beans on toast with grapefruit, baked eggs in fresh orange halves, 50 ways with sausage meat.

There is the inevitable smug feature about a woman who cooks for the famous: how Sir Alec freaked out on my egg mousse, how Dame Margot asked for more. I wish they'd tell the truth occasionally: How Harold Wilson drenched my kidneys with HP sauce or the time when the Duchess's dentures got lodged in my fairy cakes.

This kind of magazine also gives me a terrible inferiority complex. I can't say boo to a gusset, and they're always crammed with hints on how to run up 'dernier cri' oven mits in an afternoon. I'm not too good either at 'bringing my own magic to the world of clever home-making'. Life is too short to learn new ways to rebind potato peelers.

Nor am I going to be a spoil-sport this spring season, and stop my 'rug having a good ruck' by buying a product called Anti-creep.

I am reproached, too, by those pages and pages of knitting and crochet patterns telling me how to make important slipovers for the Man In My Life, or adorable layettes for a baby collie.

Consider the lilies of the field, they toilet train not,

neither do they spin, crochet or run up oven mits.

Then there's beauty. 'Save a squeezed lemon and when you have time run it over your neck.' If you want to keep fit there are 'exercises you can do with your man.' But it's nothing to do with the Kama Sutra; just Mary Rand and her husband doing press-ups.

Women's mags, however, are not all practical advice. There's Prude's Corner — muscular Christian advice from some cricketing parson or 'consultant psychiatrist.'

'As I take my guard against the Heavenly Bowler, I often ask myself whether I am capable of facing up to one of his balls — or should I say deliveries.'

And so they can't be accused of philistinism, there's the odd quote: 'No place is more delightful than one's own fireside.' (Cicero.) Or a poem from Impatience Weak.

Bounteous Spring
The crocus choir supplants the snowdrops' ring.
And bursting buds are doing their thing.
Oh how Nature's lordly gestures
Make you want to discard your winter vesture

The gorge also rises.

But there are compensations. I adore the readers' letters: 'We have a great gran who turns sheets, makes dainty matinee coats, darns socks, last year she made a rug, and she still has time to cradle the newest babe on her well-upholstered lap.' (Oh by the way, we're thinking of having her re-covered.)

Or: 'A drop of clear nail polish in the centre of each button will keep hubby's buttons from becoming loose.' (But not alas, Hubby.) And there's the problem page: 'I was shocked and horrified to find semi-nudes in brown envelopes in the back of my husband's drawers.' (What big trousers you've got Daddy.)

Or: 'To Doubly Divided, Notts. No matter how unfair you feel fate has been to you giving you a girl's heart in a man's body, you obviously have the ability to love sincerely.'

The fiction is pure joy. There's one lovely story about two men sharing a flat-chested girl in London. 'Gregory's mouth was not as firm as my Joe's. But I was tortured by my own body — like a traitor it cried out to be loved. I learnt my lesson, I had a weakness: physical passion. I went upstairs — and put on my smartest dress, and matching shoes and accessories.'

Passion flares: 'I could think no further than the day we would be married and I would lie in Ramon's arms, and consummate our love with the fierce passion I saw in his eyes. I was sustained by the thought we were in love. What did running water matter.'

In spite of the high moral tone in all the stories, however, I did detect a slightly ambiguous note in one saga entitled: *Night of Shame*. It began: 'I put my aching feet up on the old pouffe, and lent backwards with a contented sigh.'

Waxing lyrical

Some of my best friends are poets. I would rather spend an afternoon with Chatterton or Keats than with most people of my acquaintance. I am far more excited by a shelfful of verse than a room full of people. In a way poetry takes the place of religion in my life. Instead of rushing to the Bible for comfort and inspiration I pick up a copy of Milton or Shakespeare.

I realise, however, it is a passion that lays me open to ridicule. I suppose that is why it is called po-wet-try. People consider it very soppy to be always reading poems or spouting quotations. My family, for example, used to send me up rotten when I was a child.

One of my favourite sonnets was Keats' 'On First Looking into Chapman's Homer'. But my father pointed out the bit about Stout Cortez silent upon a peak in Darien, so now I have this picture of some poor dog yapping and flattened beneath an over-weight and contemplative pioneer.

Then our next door neighbour had a ginger tom, called Hopkins, but after it was neutered, my brother christened it Gerard Unmanly . . . and so it went on. Not the sort of atmosphere where poetic natures flourished.

Despite this I have an aunt who has written a great deal of poetry and gets it published all over the place. There was considerable tut-tutting in the family circle many years ago when she circulated a poem to relations young and old, which began: 'I have raped the chambers of knowledge.'

At school we got very excited over Horatius and Sir Lancelot with his coal-black curls streaming under his helmet. And we were deeply moved by Sir Richard Grenville and the little *Revenge* — they had the same sort of giant-killer appeal as Marion Coakes and Stroller.

Then at fifteen we were unleashed on the romantic poets, and all our unidentified adolescent longings found an outlet. We weren't allowed much Byron — I think they were scared we might inquire about his private life. But we adored 'Kubla Khan', particularly the bit about: 'As if this earth in fast thick pants were breathing,' which reminded us of our blue serge gym knickers. And Shelley's 'Adonais' affected us like a fever: 'He has outsoared the shadow of our night. Envy and calumny and hate and pain . . .'

Most of the poems we learned seemed to come from Palgrave's not so *Golden Treasury*, which contains far too much Thomas Campbell and other rubbish, but no Donne. I suppose Palgrave considered him too acid and tortuous.

When I reached my typing school in Oxford, however, Donne had suddenly become wildly fashionable, and every undergraduate without fail would quote: 'Oh my America, my new-found-land,' before he pounced on one.

After leaving typing school, I worked on a local paper, and never went anywhere without clutching some volume of poetry which usually had to double up as a reporter's notebook. To this day on the title page of my copy of *The Wreck of the Deutschland* is scribbled a shorthand account of a scrap-metal theft, while underneath Auden's poem about Rimbaud and Verlaine is scrawled a policeman's evidence during a court case: 'I was proceeding along the footway when I saw the defendant sitting in a gutter. He said: "I am Humpty Dumpty, I bet you cannot put me together again," and I formed the opinion he was drunk.'

But I suppose poetry ultimately appeals most when one is in love. One husband I know says he can always tell when his wife is having an affair, because all the poetry books are suddenly horizontal on top of the shelves.

I certainly read most voraciously during my adolescence and early 20s when I was hunting for a permanent mate, and ricocheting from one disastrous love affair to another.

Only in poetry could I find appropriate expression for my ecstasy, or for my subsequent despair when things went wrong: 'Oh heart, oh, heart, if he'd but turn his head. You'd know the folly of being comforted.'

Actually I must have been a pain in the neck. 'You write wonderful letters, Jill,' I remember one stockbroker saying after receiving one of my lyrical outpourings, 'but they're awfully hard to answer.'

I confess I find it embarrassing myself when people start quoting at me, and even worse when they give me one of their poems to read. There's that terrible moment when you get to the bottom of the page, and they're watching you and you don't know if the poem's finished, or if there's more over the page. (You feel you ought to know from the sense.) So you turn over surreptitiously and find nothing, and have to pretend you're examining the quality of the paper.

I wish, too, I didn't always say: 'Gosh yes, it's wonderfully moving,' when I get to the end, even if I think it's frightful. I wish I were like Ezra Pound, who when Yeats sent him a poem, merely sent back a postcard saying: 'Putrid. E.P.'

I've always, too, been fascinated by the process of writing poetry. Does inspiration strike suddenly? How spontaneous really is the overflow of powerful feeling? We know Shakespeare never blotted a line, but did Wordsworth go charging round that Lakeland cottage, shouting: 'What the bloody hell rhymes with daffodils? Fetch me the rhyming dictionary, Dorothy.' I find it very endearing that Auden's secretary once typed the wrong adjective in a poem because she couldn't read his writing, and Auden was so delighted with the improvement he left it in.

'The chief, if not the only, aim of poetry is to delight,' wrote Dryden. And I think it's a pity that parents don't encourage their children to read poetry. In fact I think children should be forcibly introduced to it like being made to learn the piano, or having a brace on one's teeth when one is young, because it's such a joy and an advantage in later life, and it enables one to do *The Times* crossword so much quicker.

And poetry does comfort and cheer. I remember going to work one morning. I had just arrived in London, and, desperately homesick for Yorkshire, crossed in love, soaked by the rain on the way to the Tube and buffeted by commuters, I was eventually disgorged on to the platform. Opposite me on the wall was a Whitbread poster, a painting of the countryside with robins in the trees, and underneath as a caption some of Wordsworth's loveliest lines: 'Art thou the bird whom men love best. The pious bird with the scarlet breast. Our little English robin.'

And suddenly the dark dismal morning seemed full of light.

The soft red light

The thing that first knocked me out about Amsterdam, even on the coldest, greyest February day, was its beauty. The houses rise, red and grey, and seem to float swanlike above the canals. The sheen on the water is olive-green, and mallards with their brilliant emerald heads slide gravely under the bridges. If you close your eyes you can see the city peopled again by those who built it — seventeenth-century burghers in their black coats, rich from trading with the Indies. But I hadn't come to dwell on the city's architectural felicities. My husband and I were spending the weekend there to have a look at the sex scene — to see if Amsterdam really was as swinging as it makes out.

On Saturday morning we awoke to the sound of bells and rumbling trams. Seagulls flocked in a noisy white mist reminding us the sea wasn't far away. But then, nothing is very far from anything in Amsterdam. Five minutes' walk from our hotel, which was in one of the most genteel parts of the city, we had our first intimation of things to come: we stumbled on the most bizarre shop selling every kind of erotic appliance imaginable, from simulated pink rubber vaginas to dildos with teddy bears on the end; from inflatable black dolls to creams called *Erecta Absoluta*, and ticklers that looked like fishing equipment. There were also some amazing magazines with names like *Doctor Prick*, *Raw Hide* and *Common Orgasm Market*. But perhaps the one that most aptly summed up the jolly atmosphere of the district was called *Tum Tum*. On its cover a girl in red boots with considerable mammalian charms was doing

63

some unmentionable things to Father Christmas.

Outside the shop, boards were cluttered with cards offering services: 'Joyce, 30, specialises in pleasant tidy gentlemen with small members'; 'Annie loves giving surprises under the shower — or simply with a cup of coffee'; and 'Girls required for Sex Club: contact Dr Utanus.'

A hundred yards on, near the Central Station, we found the Zeedijk district — the red light area itself. It is centred along the Oz Voorburgwal and the Oudezijds Achterburgwal and the small streets and bridges that link and run off them.

Apparently there are between seven and eight hundred prostitutes working here. Prices start at 15 guilders and run to 75. Girls pay about 80 a day for their rooms and taxes of up to 18,000 guilders a year (well over £2,500), so it's essential for them to pack in the customers: authorities reckon up to 20 a day. It is hardly surprising, therefore, that girls smile at you from doorways and street corners everywhere, and even pursue you on bicycles!

Most of the ones we saw were sitting in windows in various states of undress — some extremely pretty and slim, with beautiful complexions and shining clean hair, were showing so much bare thigh and bosom that they should have caught their death of cold on such a frosty day. Others, much older — more the Mae West type — sat pulling back bright mauve net curtains, smiling knowingly and crossing and recrossing varicose-veined legs. One thought instinctively of Eliot:

Grishkin is nice, her Russian eye
Is underlined for emphasis,
Uncorsetted, her friendly bust
Gives promise of pneumatic bliss.

In one doorway, a tall, tough-looking girl — six feet two of irresistible femininity — stood eating a mammoth plate of spaghetti. Obviously taking a lunch-break.

Through the windows, red-tasselled lamp-shades threw a rose-coloured glow on beds strewn with teddy bears, dolls in frilly dresses and alligators in red satin mini-skirts. Half-bras in black lace, red petticoats, leopard skin g-strings — all the *demi-monde* detritus — dripped from the ceilings. A nice touch is the driving mirrors either side of the windows, outside, so the inmates can see if anyone is hanging around nervously in need of a bit of encouragement.

In front of one house a queue of very self-conscious looking men straggled unevenly. 'That's a very popular prostitute,' we were told. Next door, appropriately enough, was a pram shop!

Under a business sign 'Haard Dolie', a boot-faced girl wrapped in fur glowered above the cigarette which hung from her drooping red mouth. Her eyes ran over us without interest — like a man reading a newspaper and skipping the woman's page as he knows it has nothing to offer him.

As it was Saturday, the Sex Museum was closed, but nearby was a shop selling nothing but binoculars. Amsterdam seems to cater for every taste. One of the most endearing things about the city, in fact, is the atmosphere of *laissez-faire* and tolerance. Leaving the Achterburgwal and the Voorburgwal, one was amazed to find the red light district curling like a snug fur collar around the lovely old church — Oude Kerk — which dates back to the thirteenth century.

Here brothels were flanked incongruously by a children's school, the Y.M.C.A., the Amsterdam Stock Exchange, and a prayer-meeting house. This intermingling of sacred and profane, of sordid and sublime, is taken completely for granted. In Amsterdam, the needs of the flesh are recognised as much as the needs of the spirit. The bells toll the quarter hours, and the girls peddle their wares in the shadow of the church.

Amsterdam is also the city on which Camus based his great novel *The Fall*, in which he wrote, 'A single sentence will suffice for modern man; he fornicated and read the papers'. Oddly enough, as we walked back to lunch, we could see the Dutch in every café avidly reading newspapers.

Evening in Amsterdam. A mist rose from the canals as we made our second trip to the Red Light District. Everything was coming to life now, the tarts doing a really brisk business, and neon signs everywhere screaming: 'Sound Union', '½ a Kip', and 'Wynand Fockink.'

We walked down a street where for one guilder you could see a fat blonde removing her clothes and writhing on a bed; past food shops selling king-sized boxes of chocolates and huge phallic-looking sausages. The sex shops were once more in evidence peddling whips, black rubber gear and sadistic magazines called *Viking* and *Bitch* in which girls with expressions of faked anguish lay with ropes biting into their plump flesh. There were also homosexual magazines showing wet-looking youths with white squares covering their private parts like Band Aid. And the inevitable rows of ads: 'Young housewife seeks part-time work'; 'Two nice girls look for variations.'

We had a drink in one of the bars frequented by the prostitutes. It looked very proper except for a few red lamps over the tables and, in fact, respectable middle-class families were also having dinner there. In one corner sat a couple who looked rigidly disapproving; the woman, my husband pointed out, was the spitting image of Mrs Whitehouse.

I had a go at interviewing some of the prostitutes. One of them, a huge blonde putting a severe strain on a sequined sweater, was happily getting drunk. She had a pouting pink mouth and heavily mascara-ed seen-it-all-before eyes. For a consideration, she said, she would be very happy to give me an interview. Then her boyfriend, an evil looking brute with black sideboards who was standing nearby, slapped a large red hand down hard on the bar and said she wasn't to talk to us.

At this, she bridled. He whispered something short and sharp in her ear and she turned pale, mumbling that she wasn't interested. They both left. 'He's the local butcher,' said the barman, 'an ugly customer.' 'He'd have made mincemeat out of you,' said my husband.

The next girl we accosted also said she would be happy to

give an interview, but for 2000 guilders (approximately £25) for a quarter of an hour — four times as much as she'd charge her customers for giving them a good time. My husband said he wouldn't mind being given a good time for 50 guilders and asking a few pertinent questions between bouts of passion — but I was against the idea.

'Plumbers and electricians,' the barman told us, 'always get a discount from the prostitutes.'

A Salvation Army lady came in jangling her tin for money. They pop up in every pub in Amsterdam, and evidently give an annual dinner for the tarts which about ten per cent attend.

Outside the bar the cross on top of the church spire shone a brilliant neon red. By moonlight, the houses have no substance and the ancient street lamps with their Boy Scout hat tops and ivy pattern winding up the stem cast daggers of light along the canal.

Next we decided to look at some blue films: '100 per cent porno guarantee', 'Real focky, focky, 35 guilders'; 'Porno bar 10 guilders'; 'Real live natural belly dances'. Men with hot eyes and greasy black curls beckoned from the doorways.

We were a party of four and finally we chose a small, sleazy dive that promised us the works for ten guilders each. In a theatre that could have housed fifty people, we found five drunk Americans in woolly hats.

'It fills up later in the evening,' said the doorman.

'Haven't been to the pictures for ages,' said my husband.

We were all in very high spirits.

The film, which was of such poor quality it looked as though it was raining all the time, showed a very pretty blonde tied up and writhing unconvincingly as an equally pretty brunette flogged her with horse hair. Cut, very suddenly, to an office with black-leather chairs. A man in a bowler hat and suit undressed to his underpants, whereupon the brunette walked in and stripped to her suspender belt. A tabby cat — it *must* have been a Civil Service office — looked on in intense embarrassment. Back to the blonde still writhing and tied to her pole. Enter a very handsome man in fur coat carrying a lighted cigar. He was just about to apply this to her left nipple when the executive in his underpants rushed in from his office, shot the man in the fur coat, set free the blonde and embraced her.

The second feature was more in the Tom Jones *genre*. A highwayman in a tricorne hat and knee-breeches drew up at a pub called the Half Way In (howls of approval greeted this). The innkeeper, who was on his last legs, had a beautiful daughter who sat around in a mob cap and licking her lips. Over supper the old father took precisely 1½ seconds to drink himself under the table, at which point the daughter stripped down to her mob cap and lured the highwayman into the nearest fourposter.

Two anachronisms brought even louder howls of joy from the audience — her well-defined bikini marks and the electric log fire.

Morning came and the highwayman and the girl were still at it. It was only at the end when our hero, aged twenty years, staggered off gland in hand into the sunrise, that we realised the girl was supposed to be twins, and he'd been attempting to satisfy them both.

Next, we all went upstairs to see the live shows. In another small theatre the curtains were drawn back to show a low bed and a picture of two windmills on the wall. Music started pounding out of the ceiling. We sat . . . and waited and waited and waited.

'Someone's forgotten their parts,' said one of the Americans.

At last, a pretty but emaciated girl with slanting eyes and black curls came undulating onto the stage wearing skin-tight red trousers and a purple velvet top. After stroking her body rather half-heartedly, she took off her sweater to reveal a beige Mary Quant bra, then, after a lot of play with her zip, removed her trousers. She was a pretty straight actress altogether.

'The plot sickens,' said my husband.

On came her sparring partner, a mettlesome looking Italian type with a black Afro and pirate's face, and a Star of David hanging round his neck. The girl proceeded to strip off his clothes down to a pair of royal blue underpants. After more writhing, she removed them too. It was totally unerotic. I sat on the edge of my seat in miserable suspense in case anyone laughed at them. It was like watching one of one's relations making an idiot of himself playing Hamlet in an amateur production.

Next they pretended to copulate in various different positions on the bed. Talk about the Dutch non-Connection.

'*I can't believe in It — any more, it's an illusion,*' sang Roger Whittaker.

It certainly was.

Gradually the girl started threshing her head back and forth as though she's got meningitis, and the man started to curl his toes up and clutch at the counterpane.

'*If that's not loving me,*' crooned Andy Williams.

'It isn't,' said one of the Americans. His mates guffawed.

'They're not even in counterpoint,' said a member of our party in a bored voice.

Finally the man grunted and groaned and collapsed in final and totally faked orgasm. The curtain drew to desultory catcalling.

'And if you think you can do better,' shouted the girl in perfect English, 'why not come up and try.' Obviously, the effect of the whole show was not at all what one might have hoped. It threw the most appalling gloom over the audience. We shuffled out in deathly silence, muttering self-consciously about where we were going to eat. All the kick had gone out of us.

Morale was only restored by an excellent dinner at the Five Flies (known in Amsterdam as the Zip). Like the Minotaur's cave inside, it has old beamed dining rooms on every level. The heavy old oak chairs have brass nameplates to show what famous people have sat on them to eat there. I sat on Michael Redgrave, my husband on Linda Christian.

Half past one. We took a last look at the red light district. It was just like Eliot again:

The street lamp said
Regard that woman
Who hesitates towards you in the light of
   the door
Which opens on her like a grin . . .
And you see the corner of her eye
Twists like a crooked pin.

Since Amsterdam is a seaport, trade goes on all round the clock. The mist had thickened, sleepy porters admitted sleepy guests, and now and then a ship hooted far off in the dark.

In the morning at the airport we were amused to see a sign that said, 'Baggage department permanently closed'. Presumably all the baggages were peddling their wares in the Zeedijk district?

Fog delayed our plane several hours and we sat around playing 'Spot the Nationality'. Suddenly over the tannoy came an announcement: 'Would Mrs Whitehouse please report to the BOAC desk.'

You could immediately tell who was English by the way they all rocked with laughter. Perhaps, after all, it *had* been the celebrated lady herself looking on so disapprovingly in the prostitutes bar!

At sevens

Having assumed the rugger season was over by May, I was very sour about going to the Sevens last week.

'You'll love it,' said my husband placatingly, 'they only play seven minutes each way.'

'That's nice,' I said cheering up, 'it'll be over in quarter of an hour.'

'Oh no,' he said happily, 'it's a knock-out, goes on for at least six hours.'

Entering Twickenham, we drove through some gates labelled Rugby Foot on one side, and Ball Union on the other. Inside a vast Middle Class Eat-In was taking place. Hearties in blazers gnawing chickenbones, swilling beer and tugging at zips which kept descending over their spreading stomachs. Their women in peaked caps with purple-veined cheeks and tunics over their bottoms, brisked about, giving the Tupperware a day out.

'I must know at least five hundred people here, Enid,' boasted a man in a flat cap to his girlfriend.

Another flatcap came and slapped him on the back.

'Hullo sport.'

'Hullo old boy.'

'How are you?'

'How are *you*?'

'See you later in the bar.'

'Who the hell's that,' said Enid as soon as flat cap was out of earshot. 'Haven't a clue. You've got a choice of two stands, Enid.'

Threatening leaden grey cloud hung over the ground. The roar of the crowd merged with unseen overhead

71

aircraft. The pitch stretched out striped yellow, green and emerald. Twickenham looks fuller than other stadiums, everyone's broader in the shoulders and really fills up his place.

On the rare occasions I've visited the ground before, I've been in a state of nervous twitch in case England or more precisely David Duckham might lose. But the Sevens is a much more relaxed affair than an International — like Tip and Run, with all the jolly boisterous undergraduate atmosphere of a bump supper or the last night of the Proms.

As we arrived Richmond, one of my husband's old clubs, were making rather heavy weather of knocking out Upper Clapton. From the groans and raucous clamour during the game, we realised we were parked in a hotbed of Upper Clapton supporters, who, once their team was ousted, settled down to the more serious business of getting drunk and accosting every girl that passed along the gangway.

On came Rosslyn Park, one of the less smart London clubs, kicking out their legs, pointing their toes. With their red- and white-striped jerseys, and almost unnaturally brown thighs, they looked more like waiters from the Popote. The important thing evidently is to keep possession of the ball, like Pig in the Middle, throwing it to one another over the other side's heads until you see a gap and then you run like hell for the enemy line.

Even more interesting, however, was what was going on off the field. In front a row of piggies were swilling whisky, beer and wine, smashing glasses and shouting 'Roobish'.

'Later,' said one, 'we'll go out and have an enormous Chinese meal.'

At the rate they were drinking, they'd certainly be regurgitating Chop Suey over the pavement around midnight.

'I've been keeping this seat warm for you, my dear,' said one as he tackled a passing middle aged woman wearing lots of green eye-shadow.

Another woman went by with an enormous bosom inside a very tight sweater. Everyone gave her a round of applause. Silly messages kept being passed over the loud speaker.

'Richard Stillwell's fiancée says she's waiting at the West Gate for him, hope you get to her in time, Richard.'

Every few seconds, enormous men clambered over me, or walked back and forth over broken glass to the Gents. Girls, I noticed, went to the Ladies just as often, but in their case to repair their faces, slapping on pancake make-up to combat the red noses and blue cheeks produced by the cold.

My husband, who had come to watch the rugger, was getting a bit uptight at such distractions. He pointed out internationals to me: Mike Gibson, from North of Ireland, slightly old-fashioned like a Second World War flying ace, and Gerald Davies, from London Welsh, the fastest man in the game, with the black moustache, turkey-cock strut, and short darting legs, reminiscent of the dancing master in *Le Bourgeois Gentilhomme*.

Then there was the handsome Bucknall of Richmond, ex-captain of England who, like David Duckham, has perfected that special rugger-star walk, in which you stick your chest out, and straighten your leg backward with each step, to make your thighs shudder. I've always thought that tries and thighs were the better part of rugger.

In spite of lowering skies, the rain kept off. Alas the beer did not; time and again I was drenched by a shower of Courage as another Party Seven hopelessly shaken by an excited supporter, exploded on being opened. One man behind us had brought 180 pints in a keg.

Only four teams were left in now; they looked very tired, watching each other like cats, trying to whip up enthusiasm. London Welsh narrowly beat Richmond Second, Richmond First put out Gibson and North of Ireland. Ululation and view halloos accompanied every try.

Upper Clapton were getting thoroughly untinned now. Fights were breaking out. Scrumpled-up paper bags were being hurled at photographers and the touch judges. Beer trickled down from higher rows under my feet. My husband got more and more disapproving and had sharp

73

words with the piggies, who started feeding me pieces of chocolate to irritate him.

An eager woman in a red duffle coat was swept up and passed like a rugger ball along the front row. She seemed to love it, giggling hysterically, legs flailing.

'Upper Clapton's handling's much better off the field,' said a wag.

The woman's husband looked on stonily but impotently from five rows back.

During the interval before the Final, we wandered round the ground. Yet another Upper Clapton supporter lay on the concrete outside the Gents, sleeping peacefully. I suppose people drink so heavily at rugger matches as compensation. Most of them would like to be playing, but are either too old or not good enough. Or perhaps it's a defence mechanism, so that if their side loses they'll be too drunk to care.

'Way-ells. Way-ells,' came the great singing chorus of the Welsh supporters. London Welsh, winners three years running, were the stage villains of the ground, and most of them looked swarthy and mephistophelian enough to disappear through a trap door any moment in a puff of smoke. I'm fascinated how they get every member of the team with a Welsh name, I'm sure they change them by Deed Poll.

London Welsh kicked off, and were soon fooling around behind their own line, taunting Richmond, tossing the ball to one another. I was reminded of the Beatrix Potter tale in which Miss Moppet very meanly tosses the mouse about in a handkerchief.

Well Nemesis overtook London Welsh as it did Miss Moppet. One of the Richmond players snatched the ball from Gerald Davies and buried it triumphantly in the lush green grass. Three glorious tries followed, bringing the crowd howling to their feet. Richmond were now leading 24-nil and beginning to look a bit smug.

Then London Welsh, getting off their knees like a boxer on the stroke of ten, staged a magnificent comeback. Rhodri Ellis Jones, golden hair flying, shot like a rocket over the line. Two more tries followed. The stadium boiled over like a cauldron, even the piggies' jaws were stilled, and the baboons behind stopped chattering.

'Come on Richmond, come on Wales,' chanted a drunk beside me.

Then Richmond, aided by old Thunderthighs Bucknall, scored two more tries, and it was all over. The ground erupted. The entire group of Upper Clapton supporters, who'd been swaying like ships in a gale, were suddenly deposited in my lap.

The ground emptied except for the rattle of Party Sevens being kicked about. But in the bar, determined to stay in the limelight, four Upper Clapton supporters hung from the rafters, slowly removing their pants and their red and white sweaters, until they swayed with glazed eyes completely naked.

Desmond Morris, thou shouldst have been living at this hour.

Scrimping and scraping

After a spinechilling bank statement yesterday, all my energies are now centred on a major panic about money. And these panics always take the same form. Last night I sweated into the still watches planning drastic economies and a complete change of lifestyles. About 4 a.m. I woke my husband: 'I've found the answer,' I said, 'I'm going to learn to drive at once and take the car to Sainsbury's every week and stock up and then . . .'

'I know, I know,' he muttered groggily, 'we're going to forget about wine, drink nothing but cider for the next six months, and have all the cats put down,' and promptly went back to sleep again.

After a wretched night, I spent a hideous day stewing windfalls, slicing the garlic sausage thinner, trying to persuade the children to eat margarine, and making a disgustingly fatty casserole out of belly of pork, which even the dog rejected.

I even washed and ironed four double sheets. I ironed and ironed and ironed and then discovered the beastly things had been trailing in the cat's plate, so the next guest who comes to stay will be wafted to sleep on the aroma of fish skin and nourishing jellymeat Whiskas.

I also made pathetic attempts to economise on telephone calls by trying to make my conversations terse and to the point. It didn't work.

'What's up with you?' said a girl-friend, 'you sound terribly ratty.'

So I had to invite her round for a drink to placate her, which meant another sortie to the off-licence. Our drink bills, I'm afraid, are astronomical. We've always had a better eye for a bar than a bargain.

And then, of course, there's loathsome Christmas looming on the horizon waiting to take another great bite out of the budget. If I could only give up gin and Christmas for a few years, we might keep our heads above water.

But alas my economy drives never last very long. After a week of shallow baths and turning off lights, the wine and cream start creeping back into the casseroles, and things return to normal.

Another reason we're broke is that since we moved over the river, we've had to make such an effort keeping up with all the Joneses. In Fulham everyone kept to themselves, so we were able to live in complete squalor, but in Putney they're great droppers-in, so one has to keep the place clean, which means Hoovers roaring all the time eating up electricity, and vats of Gumption and Flash and Safety Brobat arriving with every delivery from the grocers. Cleanliness may be next to Godliness, but it's very expensive.

Even worse, my children keep agitating for a colour telly, claiming nobody will come to play with them if they have to watch 'Playschool' in black and white.

We're also broke because we've got hooked on the fallacy that time is money. In fact it's just a marvellous excuse to take taxis everywhere rather than buses and, instead of trailing around the shops, to have everything delivered from the most expensive retailers in the Lower Richmond Road.

At least one gets Pink Stamps. But that doesn't help much. We've collected nearly forty books of stamps since we lived here, but when they showed us the catalogue the only thing we fancied out of a sea of chromium and plastic was a goat which turned out to be one of the props in the garden-tool section.

It isn't just the housekeeping that eats into the budget. Guilt costs a bomb. Every time I feel I've been neglecting my husband or the children, I spend a fortune on surprise presents, and I always overtip. It's part of my insecurity, that awful thing of wanting everyone in the world, even taxi drivers and porters, to love me.

Our house is a Gannetorium anyway. With six people in it, the roast joint always gets wolfed in a sitting and never graduates into cold meat or shepherd's pie.

My daily — who needs constant pandering to her kitchen-beautiful whims — keeps bullying me to invest in a deep freeze, claiming it's cheaper to buy in bulk. I'm resisting like hell. Bulk buying has never done anything but increase our bulk. Nobody has any self-control. The only thing a huge fridgeful of food would encourage would be midnight feasts.

The worst thing about being broke however is it causes so much marital discord. I know my attitude to money is irrational: complete flap when we haven't got any, complete refusal to talk about it because it's so boring when we have. My husband does his best to encourage me to budget. But we have these absurd squabbles when he comes home in the evening, finds three final demands growing mouldy beneath a pile of washing, and starts lecturing me about organisation and keeping bills in one place.

If on the other hand he's been overspending, I get the typical male bull about women not understanding economics, and money being a commodity that can be bought and sold like anything else.

I know I shouldn't grumble and that millions of people are far worse off than we are. But money does seem to have become impossibly tight recently since England joined the Common Market, and the Tories started living off the VAT of the land.

It seems rather immoral, too, that on the one hand wages are frozen, yet on the other, we are bombarded with Access Cards, credit facilities, round-the-clock cash dispensers and offers of easy terms — all encouraging us to spend more money and get deeper and deeper into debt.

There must be some solution to the problem. I have pipe dreams (I wonder if Cardinals have Pope dreams) about being left a fortune or writing the great best seller. But I think the answer would be to find a bi-sexual millionaire who would fall in love with me and my husband equally and take us on jaunts and pour money into the kitty — and into the kitties too for that matter. They'd much prefer steak tartare to Whiskas.

And I suppose there is some consolation to be gained from the fact that sex is still free. After all, it does keep one away from the shops some of the time. I've always thought if you take care of the penis, the pounds will take care of themselves.

Still Olave and kicking

Olave, Lady Baden-Powell, is Chief Guide of the World. Although I had never met her, I knew lots about her, because my parents lived until recently at Hampton Court, and my mother and she used to cultivate a joint allotment at the Palace.

I remember seeing Baden-Powell's jacket flapping on the scarecrow of the allotment, and reading the wildly-typed missives Lady Baden-Powell used to send my mother, full of exclamation marks and underlining and more often than not ending up: 'Hooray, Hooray, Hoo-jolly-Ray.'

On one occasion when my mother was invited to lunch, she found herself surrounded by Guiding Top Brass from all parts of the world. As they sat down to eat, Lady B-P insisted each one stand up in turn while she introduced them, and she started round the table moving from one eager unpainted face to another: Chief Guide Mukuma from Basutoland, Chief Guide Twistleton-Cavendish from the Falklands, and so on, until finally reaching my mother, she cried out in ringing tones:

'And this is Mrs Sallitt from the allotments!'

I myself was never a Guide — I didn't approve of all those pocket knives for taking Boy Scouts out of Girl Guides — and I was sacked from the Brownies after three weeks for insubordination. It was with great trepidation therefore that on a thundery afternoon I went down to Hampton Court to talk to Lady Baden-Powell about her new book.

On the way there, to bring myself up to date with guiding

activities, I studied a copy of *The Guider*. It was full of the kind of articles which began: 'The chatter subsided and twenty-four pairs of eager eyes rested upon Brown Owl.'

Oh dear, I thought as I wandered along the rose-red Elizabethan passages leading to Lady B-P's apartments. I was ushered into a huge chintzy drawing room, the walls covered with B-P's water colours and gleaming swords from Mafeking.

Lady Baden-Powell came to meet me, and seizing my hand, gazed deeply into my eyes: 'Welcome,' she cried in a rich baritone, 'how is your dear mother? She was such a beautiful woman. Are you like her?' She looked at me consideringly, then added kindly: 'Well perhaps not, never mind, sit down, sit down.'

She talks with tremendous emphasis, her constantly rising eyebrows putting in the schoolgirl exclamation marks. At eighty-four she is still splendid looking. A junoesque figure in a blue and green paisley dress, with very white hair drawn into a bun, a freckled face, blazing brown eyes, and a huge grin that splits her face in half like Harpo Marx.

On the sofa sat two other top guides: her grand-daughter-in-law, Patience, who is jolly and pretty, and the wife of the present Lord Baden-Powell; and a 'delegate' from Geneva, who had a keen weathered face and far-seeing blue eyes. I was glad I had cleaned my shoes.

We then sat down to a pow wow and nursery tea of brown bread and Marmite and chocolate biscuits. Lady Baden-Powell said her family had encouraged her to write the book: 'The title comes from an awfully good poem by Patience Strong.' She then spoke of her childhood, which was spent permanently on the move. Her mother was vain, beautiful and affected, her father, a charming dilettante, who in a restless search for the perfect house humped Olave and her brother and sister from one stately home to another.

Lady Baden-Powell however, revelled in the packing and unpacking. 'Olave,' wrote her mother when she was ten, 'who is the equal of three charwomen in work, and to the whole char race in wits, hurls all her sweet energy and thought into every corner.'

For the next few years, her life passed in a fierce round of tennis parties, hunting, doting on her pets, playing the violin, being bored by *The Importance of Being Earnest*, and going to dances.

'I am fizzing with excitement about the week after next,' she had written in her diary about her coming-out dance.

'But I felt I was wasting my life,' said Lady Baden-Powell, helping herself to more bread and Marmite. 'Three young men proposed to me, but I didn't care for any of them. I had an enormous capacity for love but no outlet except my dogs and my horses. Then my father took me on a Caribbean cruise.'

On board was Robert Baden-Powell, hero of Mafeking, founder of Scouting, and confirmed bachelor. But even though he was fifty-five years old — thirty-two years Olave's senior, it was instant infatuation for both of them.

'Normally I was shy,' said Lady Baden-Powell, 'but at our first meeting there was no problem.'

'We've met before?' Baden-Powell said musingly.

'You live in London, you have a brown-and-white spaniel,' he went on. Two years before he had seen Olave walking her dog, Doogy, across Hyde Park, and had been particularly impressed by her 'quick determined gait, indicative of honesty of purpose, common sense, as well as a spirit of adventure.'

Five days later, they were meeting secretly on deck to exchange kisses. 'We were ecstatically in love,' said Lady Baden-Powell. But it was necessary to be circumspect. The leader of Scouting could not be indulging in shipboard philandering with a girl half his age! Olave therefore had to endure the attentions of other passengers.

Six months later, having exchanged endless love letters, Baden-Powell returned from a world Scouting tour, and they became engaged. Not everyone was delighted.

'My mother had hysterics,' said Lady Baden-Powell, 'Robin (as she calls him) was too old and too poor.' Nor it seems were the Scouts overjoyed: 'I am dreadfully disappointed in you,' wrote one small Scout, 'I have often thought to myself how glad I am the Chief Scout is not married because if he was he could never do all those ripping things for boys, and now you're going to do it. I think it's awfully selfish of you.'

He need not have worried. Baden-Powell carried on Scouting and Olave threw herself into Guiding activities after she was married with all the fervour of a neophyte.

'I was always naturally kind and helpful,' she said. 'Now all the longing for a purpose in life had at last found an outlet.'

From then on life was a triumphal round of globe trotting, speech making, spreading the message of the 'Movement.' 'Tea for 400 Scouts on the lawn — so jolly,' she writes in her diary one day.

If Olave had not existed, Sir John Betjeman would certainly have invented her.

Had it not been difficult at twenty-three years old adjusting to a man of fifty-five, who had never had anything to do with women?

Lady Baden-Powell shook her head violently.

'Never, never, we were always blissfully happy, never a cross word. We felt exactly the same age,' she said.

'Grandfather never grew up,' muttered Patience Baden-Powell from the depths of the sofa.

Olave and Baden-Powell certainly shared one adolescent passion of giving everything nicknames.

'We called our Rolls-Royce "Jam Roll," my typewriter was "Beetle," my attaché case L.J. because it went on Long Journeys.

'He excelled at everything,' she went on dreamily, 'painting, writing, acting, riding.'

'He must have ridden a lot at Mafeking,' said Patience.

'Nonsense,' said Lady B-P, 'they didn't ride horses at Mafeking, they ate 'em.'

Although Olave was devastated by Baden-Powell's death in 1941, and even thought about suicide, she still carried on Guiding until recently when ill-health forced her to give up.

Guiding, Lady Baden-Powell said, her voice taking on a messianic ring, has never been in a more thriving state than now. With three-quarters of a million Guides in England, recruiting figures were rising all the time. As she spoke of 'the unique sacrifice of guiding leaders around the world,' she looked sharply across at me to see that I was getting it all down.

Remembering a rather dubious slogan of one Guide division: 'Please give a shilling to a Guide who is willing,' I asked her how Guiding coped with the permissive society.

'Did you come down here by Green Line?' asked Lady Baden-Powell.

'I'm slowing down now,' said Lady Baden-Powell. 'I don't involve myself with meetings or HQ affairs any more. But I type letters, I keep in touch in black and white. This year I sent more than 2,000 Christmas cards.'

A great wave of depression swept over her. She looked down unseeingly at the freckles on the back of her hands. 'As long as I can still be of use, that's all that matters in life. But I long for the end — so I can be united with Robin again.'

An overgrown schoolgirl she may be, but what one remembers is the warmth, the magnetism, the cheerfulness and above all the guts. I thought of Empson's poem to an Old Lady.

'Ripeness is all. Her in her cooling planet revere.'

Motherly afflictions

As I ramble past the cemetery on Putney Common with the dog bounding irreverently in and out of the gravestones, one epitaph always catches my eye.

'*Jane Selwyn died 1889 — a devoted mother, her children arise and call her blessed.*'

And I start wondering if the stonemasons will ever chisel such pleasantries on my tombstone. I rather doubt it.

I like to be a good mother. But it never seems to work that way with me. My children are angelic when they're asleep, and when my husband's there, but when I take them out on my own, they always seem to play up, running riot in Biba or letting water pistols loose on old ladies.

I took my son to the doctor yesterday. 'I'm terribly sorry to bother you,' I said with my usual string of apologies, 'but he's been boiling hot and he hasn't eaten for two days.' 'And I'm very hungry now,' announced my son beaming.

You shouldn't spoil them, says my husband. I know, I know. But Emily, my daughter, has reached the stage when she wants to walk everywhere but refuses to hold my hand. The only way to keep her in her pram is bribery.

'I will not weaken,' I mutter grimly, as I trundle past the first sweet shop to the accompanying wails of 'lollies', 'sweeties.'

Come the second sweet shop, I invariably give in. Peace is restored with a large ice cream. Today, I tell myself guiltily, my sanity is more vital than Emily's character. Tomorrow I'll start saying no.

Then there are those dreadful afternoons when it's only three o'clock and pouring with rain, and there's no one for

85

them to play with because all their friends are away. I turn into an instant fishwife. All I seem to be doing is screaming, and shouting: 'Stop it!' But the noise gets louder and louder, until finally it's tears before nightfall — usually mine. Whereupon there's a complete and shaming role reversal.

My daughter rushes over and starts patting me on the shoulder and saying sorry, and my son tries to placate me with a present.

Last week he consoled me with one of his Snap cards.

'What's the good of one lousy playing card?' I sniffed grudgingly.

'It's very good for picking your teeth,' said my son.

Then suddenly, in the middle of the night, the fishwife's remorse strikes (it should be turned into an opera by Benjamin Britten) when I wake up in a cold sweat and decide I'm ruining my children in their formative years, and all they'll remember when they grow up is my shouting at them. Comes the dawn, and still racked with doubt, I listen with blessed relief to the banging and singing upstairs as two apparently undamaged children greet a new day.

It's all to do with their ages, say kind friends. My son, being four, has reached the 'why' to everything stage, and my daughter at two wants to have long conversations about half of which I understand. It's rather like having to talk French all day, and just as exhausting.

I think the trouble with our house is that too many people need a devoted mother. 'I never see you these days,' grumbles my husband. And the cats are so edgy since the dog arrived, that I've had to evolve a stroking rota.

I thought it would be such a nice country atmosphere for the children if they were brought up with lots of animals — but all it means is discipline goes to pot at mealtimes.

How can I ensure my children eat up, when the dog is hanging around like a great grinning waste disposal unit, and the minute I look round, I'm confronted by two totally clean plates, and three innocent faces, except that the dog's cheeks are bulging with cold sprouts and pieces of sausage?

I don't even seem to have made a success of teaching my children the facts of life. I do try. But when I went upstairs the other day, I found my son cavorting round wearing a pair of my tights with two volumes of Scott tucked in the front. My daughter lay on a sheet on the sofa giggling.

'What are you both doing?' I said.

'We're playing fathers and daddies,' said my son.

Gay Lib strikes again.

I suppose, too, devoted mothers play with their children more than I do.

I like reading to them and telling them stories, but I really draw the line at Lego. My hands shake too much. Someone gave my son a huge box recently, and the house is now strewn with windowless bungalows — like an aftermath of the Bomb.

'It ought to be called Sore Footo, rather than Lego,' muttered my husband, as he staggered groggily out of bed this morning, treading hard on a half-built windmill.

But the thing I feel most Angst-ridden about is not taking enough interest in my children's education. I glaze at dinner parties when the trendies start grumbling about this and Thatcher and the merits of the State system.

You know the sort of thing.

'I wouldn't dream of letting Gideon go to a State school, and be jostled by all those rough children, besides they never push them enough.'

Equally depressing are the people who rush round putting foetuses down for Winchester or Cranbourne Chase.

My children aren't down for anywhere. My son has just gone to the local primary school, which he refers to as All Scents. He adores it and he seems to enjoy all the 'jostling of the rough children.'

However, even that brought problems. There was no more rolling up at 10.30 like we used to at the Playgroup when I had a hangover or overslept. The whistle goes promptly at 9.15.

Then there's the trauma of dinner money, 12p actually, to be found every day. I wanted to write a cheque, but evidently that's bad for discipline, so most mornings there's the same rat race of turning out piggy banks.

And I did hope at last the dreadful one-up-childship would let up but it hasn't. Where it used to be: 'Isn't he walking, talking, out of nappies yet?' it is now, 'Gideon can read and write and count up to a thousand, how about yours?'

'Oh I don't bother about that sort of thing,' I lie airily.

Untrue, untrue. You should see me addressing birthday cards from my son. Carefully putting the pen in my left hand to write: 'Love from Felix,' even putting the F in backwards to make the whole thing look more authentic.

'Parents,' said Anthony Powell, 'are sometimes a bit of a disappointment to their children. They seldom fulfil the promises of their early years.'

I would like to be a devoted mother . . . but I do like a bit of peace sometimes . . . at least I think I do. My girlfriend has taken the children out for the day so I can work. My husband and the dog have gone to play cricket, and the house seems strangely quiet and empty. I must say I miss them all dreadfully . . . .

No nudes is bad nudes

I must confess I enjoy looking at photographs of naked women. I often find them aesthetically pleasing, and I like to see how they differ in shape from myself. That one's much fatter than me, I think smugly. Or, I wonder if I'd look as good as this one — given decent lighting, air conditioner to stiffen the nipples, and a few strategically placed teddy bears:

Male nudes are another matter. I remember a girlfriend going to see a gynaecologist, because she was having trouble starting a baby.

'You love your husband,' said the gynaecologist, 'but when you see him with nothing on, do you think Grrrrrrrrr?' 'No,' said my girlfriend, she didn't.

'That's why you're not conceiving,' said the gynaecologist triumphantly.

I think he was talking absolute tripe. Men may be turned on by the sight of naked girls: But I don't believe that the Grrr factor exists for women. I'm not at all excited seeing men in the nude, particularly in photographs. They look so vulnerable and self-conscious and that isn't erotic at all. Organs — except playing Bach — move me not one jot.

All the same it must have been dreadful living in Victorian times and never seeing one's partner naked, or always making love in the dark.

I remember being impressed by a story of a woman who used to welcome her husband home from work by opening the front door stark naked. So I tried it myself.

It was not a success. My husband got home so late that I played the piano to fill in the time, and when he eventually arrived, I greeted him blue with cold, and with a wicker-work bottom.

People have very strange attitudes to nudity. I can't understand parents who always shrink from letting their children see them with nothing on. The children must have the shock of their lives when they grow up and first confront someone in the nude. One man I know said the first time he saw a naked woman was when he was eighteen, and living in a boarding house. The geyser exploded in the bathroom, and one of the female lodgers rushed out not only naked but also minus her eyebrows.

As a child, of course, one didn't really associate nudity with eroticism. At school when I was eleven, I remember coming across an upper class divorce scandal in the paper in which a Duke and his mistress had taken snapshots of each other with nothing on. My only reaction was: what a soppy thing to do.

One friend of ours bent on immortalising his wife in the buff got hold of a Polaroid camera recently. But it was a disaster, he said. The flash went wrong, and she came out with bright red eyes looking like an eager Women's Institute rat. Another time they took photographs of each other on holiday. But Kodak refused to co-operate. They sent back prints of the wife looking very Health and Efficiency, but kept the negatives of the husband saying he was unsuitable for reproduction. Odd . . . he already had three children.

Whether one minds taking off one's clothes or not has a lot to do with feeling fat. Seven pounds lighter with an all-over mahogany suntan, I might consider flaunting myself over a gatefold, but they'd have to pay me a million pounds before I posed after Christmas dinner.

One notices too men with good torsos are always whipping off their shirts at the first pale shaft of sunlight. And as Atticus pointed out earlier this year, although Onassis blew his top in public over the nude photographs of Jackie, he was secretly delighted because she looked so good in them.

It seems illogical to me that the Festival of Light makes such a fuss about pubic hair in photographs, when it's considered quite all right in paintings — even though it's probably taken the artist far longer lovingly to paint in each hair, than for the photographer to press a button.

The trouble is we've all got rather blasé about nudity these days. It seems to be everywhere: in films, theatres, deodorant ads — though admittedly they haven't got it on the wireless yet. If Lady Godiva rode naked through Coventry today, I doubt if Peeping Tom would leave his television set.

And, finally, it is refreshing that there are still people who find nudity slightly embarrassing. A friend of mine who was wrapped in a towel and hastily putting out the dustbins the other day, was appalled when an enormous dustman seized not only the dustbin but the towel as well.

And I am reminded of the story of a Master of Fox-hounds who asked a friend back to tea after a drenching day's hunting. A true gentleman, he offered the friend a fresh set of clothes and his dressingroom to change in.

After a hot bath, the friend was standing naked in the dressingroom sliding one of the MFH's shirts over his head, when the MFH's wife came into the room, and seizing part of him cried: 'Ding ding, darling, tea's ready.'

The poor lady was horrified when she went downstairs to find her husband standing in front of the drawing-room fire.

Having a lovely war

I must confess I enjoyed the war — I was two when it began. I didn't even mind the economies — eating delicious spinach made from young nettles and making one's weekly treat of a boiled egg last for at least six pieces of toast.

I also have dim memories of my mother singing at the top of her voice with wild happiness after my father telephoned to say he was safely back from Dunkirk. The tobacco plants were in flower and since then whenever I catch a whiff of that sweet heady scent, it triggers off instant euphoria. We were almost as excited when my father returned in 1943 from America bringing the first oranges my brother and I had ever tasted.

Although my mother seemed more frightened of the local air raid warden than the Germans, the bombs fell fairly regularly. One dropped as we were about to bathe in the river. We all flattened ourselves in the wild garlic, except two of my little friends who prostrated themselves in a bed of thistles, which caused more tears than the subsequent explosion.

Another bomb fell on my school. It was during lunch. All the windows blew in, filling the orange jelly we were eating with pieces of glass. Within minutes hoards of mothers, like the Ride of the Valkyries, converged from all sides bicycling frenziedly. Fortunately none of their darlings was hurt, but school was closed for three months — one of my first intimations that the Germans might be on my side.

And when it was all over, there were parties with bonfires and bunting, where we burnt Hitler's effigy and got frightful indigestion from eating baked potatoes that hadn't quite cooked in the ashes.

It all seemed a great lark, and says much for the stiff upper lips of my parents that none of their anxiety was transmitted to their children. One of the less attractive aspects of war, however, is that as it recedes, its horrors recede too, and it is with growing alarm that I notice its increasing popularity at the moment. With *The Regiment*, *The World at War* and *Colditz* it seems to me that war is no longer regarded as an instrument of mass murder, but as something rather glamorous they do amazingly well on television.

A schoolmistress told me recently that all but one of her class of six-year-olds are allowed to stay up to watch *Colditz*, and it's not just the boys who are hooked. Since Princess Anne married a handsome dragoon, all the girls are, apparently, determined to land an Army officer. The other day I even heard a colleague's wife who gets everything wrong, boasting how pleased she was her son was 'going into the Greens.'

Another indication of war mania is doubled attendance figures at the Imperial War Museum, which I visited last week.

'Duddy, Duddy, come 'ere.'

'What is it Jason?'

'What's the difference between a male tank and a female tank?'

The Dads of course were having a field day, growing in stature every second, regurgitating the smattering of inaccurate information they'd gleaned during National Service. Older men with neat moustaches, very straight backs and copies of the *Daily Telegraph*, looked with ill concealed disapproval at long-haired youths in anoraks with loud laughs. Perhaps they were suffering from Anoraksia Nervosa.

Small boys crowded round models of battles, pressed buttons to make Allied countries light up on maps, and gazed into the sad mad eyes of Gavrilo Princip. There were typically English inventions — gas-proof kennels for dogs, and gas-masks for horses — and a full-size doodlebug looking rusty and harmless. It was hard to believe they destroyed most of the houses in Croydon and places like that.

It was also hard to believe, looking at blown-up photographs of a Nazi Rally with miles of helmets spreading out like a vast iron cornfield, that we ever managed to win the war. But reading the details of the German surrender, it was impossible not to feel delighted that we did. After the Eurovision Song Contest, and Saturday's débâcle at Twickenham, it's such a nice change to be on the winning side.

Next door was the VC room. There was something oddly similar about those reckless flamboyant young men, smiling in their cockpits like racing drivers, with their straight noses, off-centre partings, and remote detached look about the eyes, as though they knew well that death was waiting on the horizon. But how brave they were!

'Those men,' said the caption, 'fought with emotion and impetuosity, never considering the odds against them, but relying on superlative flying skill. They waited in the sky until a formation appeared, then exploiting speed and surprise would dive upon their opponents.'

Then there was Violette Szabo, posthumous winner of the George Cross, 'placed in solitary confinement, who although continually and atrociously tortured, refused to betray the secrets of her country'.

People like her always make me feel so dreadfully ashamed, knowing quite well that I would tell all the moment the first match was rammed under my toe-nail. I suppose, though, that most men feel the same, and part of the lure of war is the worry whether one would be gallant and brave enough, or whether one would go to pieces, under fire. There must be a horrifying moth-to-the flame desire to put oneself to the test.

One of the museum's most beautiful exhibits is all Allenby's medals, rows and rows of them, pale-blue striped with flame, old-rose with grey, like rosettes in a show jumper's tackroom.

'We try not to dwell too much on the glories of war,' said

Noble Frankland, the enlightened director of the museum. 'We aim to present an impartial view of every aspect of war. But if, on the other hand, we emphasised the grisly aspect too much, we'd be accused of giving the children nightmares.

'I think it's important for children to come to terms with their own instincts. Our aim is to counteract the fictionalised violence of war on television.'

Two small boys stopped in their tracks in front of a large and wonderfully handsome photograph of General Alexander.

'That bloke was in the last instalment of *Colditz*,' said one.

'Yeah, you're right,' said the second.

Looking at the splendid uniforms, the coloured medals, and the records of glorious achievement, one sees war in all its heraldry and beauty. It is easy to forget while someone was acting gloriously, someone else was usually dying horribly.

At the top of the stairs is a painting of lounging diplomats with bland pink untroubled faces, drawing up a peace treaty. Next door in appalling contrast, is 'Gassed,' Sargent's huge nightmare painting of an advanced dressing station in 1918.

A file of soldiers, hands on each other's shoulders, heads bowed, eyes bandaged, stumble in a ghastly line over the dead and dying bodies of their comrades. A similar file shuffles towards them from the right. In between rises the full moon that many of them will never see again. Nothing could bring home more forcefully the futility, horror and poignancy of war.

Yet in the next room, almost as an act of absolution, is displayed a collection of the first wild flowers to bloom again on the devastated areas of the Somme: Herb Robert, Traveller's Joy, Self Heal and Forget-me-not, homely weeds yet symbols of the resilience of nature and the human spirit.

As Liddell Hart pointed out: 'If you wish for peace, you must first understand war.'

Going to the dogs

Much of my youth was spent hawking our long-suffering golden retriever round local dog shows. He never won, except fourth prize once when there were only four dogs in the class, and he loathed every minute of it. To avenge himself, he invariably escaped during the show and had to be paged over the loud speaker. 'Will the owner of Dog No . . . currently demolishing the Fancy Gâteaux Stall . . .' It was with nostalgia, therefore, that I visited Cruft's last week.

A smell of hot dog and hair lacquer hung on the foetid Olympia air. Everywhere there were rows of dogs on benches, sleeping, yawning, looking wistful, sprawled on fur rugs or candlewick counterpanes. Frenzied grooming was going on. If you have hairs to shed, prepare to shed them now.

In one corner there were briards — French Dougal dogs — all bouncing and peering through fringed curtains of hair. In another, cavalier spaniels lay exquisitely beautiful in liquid heaps. In another chows with black tongues and hangover frowns looked as though they had been at the red wine last night. Great Danes stood gentle and faintly apologetic like very tall girls at cocktail parties.

'How many dogs have you got, now, Lilian?'

'Oh we're down to fifteen at the moment.'

The exhibitors were even more remarkable than their dogs. They fell into two distinct types: public-bar men with short Brylcreemed hair parted in the middle, very red necks, tattooed arms, and fake sheepskin coats; and grizzled middle-class ladies with cropped hair, red veins, gin-soaked voices, cigarettes slotted into their lower lips, and massive trousered bottoms.

A doberman class was in progress. A great deal of doggery pokery going on. Even during the judging, exhibitors could not stop fiddling with their dogs, pulling out their legs, tugging them off the ground by non-existent tails, snapping fingers, brandishing hairbrushes and cloths to catch any trace of slobber. It was all very uncool — rather like lipsticking in public.

The fun really began when the dogs had to show off their paces, and each elephantine lady owner ran round the ring, pearls bouncing and falling on her vast twin-setted bosom.

The judges, clad in a little brief authority and tweed skirts, came straight out of the staff room, as they stumped briskly round the ring, squatting down to look at the exhibits like golfers examining the lie of a putt.

The best five dogs were lined up nose to tail. Second was moved up to first place. Prizes were handed out. Firm handshakes exchanged. Dog number three, with understandable irritation, lost his temper and bit the winner. Fur and expletives were soon flying, dogs and cameramen snapping, as the two owners tore their dogs apart.

'Oh please,' cried a girl reporter, scribbling frantically, 'would you mind repeating the last sentence?'

They did — and she turned very pink.

At the edge of the ring, a lady in a pork-pie hat brandished a bulldog-clipped petition. 'Exhibitors in favour of the retaining of docking, please sign here,' she said in a ringing voice.

Obedience classes were also in progress. Owners striding briskly up and down, like bowlers pacing out their runs, dogs following their owners like shadows, anxious eyes trying to read their minds. An Alsatian sat by itself in the ring for 10 minutes — one of the tests — trembling with nerves, and licking its lips like a starlet interviewed on telly.

Around the hall were stalls with very smooth men flogging dog products: clipping devices, high protein low calorie dog biscuits, vaginal deodorants for bitches, Mr

Groom — they have such absurd names. I always feel an idiot in the local grocer asking for four large Pals, and two small Chums.

Do people really grow to look like their dogs? Certainly people who own the same breed tend to look like each other. The poodle ladies, for example, were very done up with lots of turquoise eye shadow, white boots, spangles in their spunglass hair, and cupid's-bow mouths bearing no relation to the thinness of their lips. But over on the Alsatian benches, it was all whine, women and throng, tough ladies in leather with very dyed black hair, who looked as though they spent their time writing letters to *Forum* on the delights of corporal punishment. Next door, the Great Danes seemed mostly to be manned by tweedy women with Continental-shelf bosoms.

It was lunchtime. The Brylcreem brigade ate Spam and beetroot sandwiches. The large grizzled ladies tucked into pork pies, washed down with large nips of gin. I suppose if you're disappointed in men you turn to dogs, who give you uncritical adoration whether your hips spread or not.

A little girl slept on a sleeping mastiff, a copy of *Squirrel Nutkin* lying open in her hands. Several dogs were covered in netting like raspberries to ward off the public.

'By the end of the day,' explained an owner, 'the dogs have got flat heads. Some dogs take to it, some don't.'

The heat was becoming too much for the St. Bernards. One got bored and launched himself off his bench like a great liner going into the water. It took three people to heave him back again. He had a flowered towel tied like a bib under his chin to stop him drooling.

'Quick, the graduate bitches are going into the ring.' I never knew dogs got degrees. B. Litters, I suppose.

Toys were upstairs rather like Boots the Chemist. Here tweeness reigned supreme, every toy dog sitting in a cage hung with curtains in tartan, flowered chintz or velvet.

'My doggy loves to be surrounded by beauty,' said a peke owner, giving the dog little bits of turkey with fat heavily ringed fingers.

I left suffering from a fit of peke.

Downstairs delicious Pyrenean mountain dogs shuffled round like animated fur rugs. One edged towards a row of picnicking teenagers and slyly helped himself to a sandwich. With total disregard to Crufts Rule 28 about no bitches being mated on the precincts, one dog climbed laboriously on top of another.

Yet I must confess, as a biased setter owner, that I found most delectable of all the rows of English setters — lovely freckled heads lolling, plumed tails swinging. Groucho Marx eyebrows shooting up and down. Once in the ring they turned it into a great cockleg party: snuffling, goosing, gambolling, beseeching the judge to join in their silly setter games.

'I gave mine a great clout beforehand,' said a winning owner, 'so she behaved herself. She likes winning anyway.'

But as I left I wondered how much the dogs really enjoy the palaver. A friend who exhibits her dog regularly said that recently before a show she bathed him in scented soap. Afterwards he gave her the slip. She found him at the bottom of the garden, digging frenziedly, dirtying himself up. When she looked to see what he was burying — it was the scented soap.

The revolt of the Putney Common dogwalkers

A splendid row has erupted in Putney. It started a few weeks ago, when a sinister notice went up announcing a meeting to discuss 'proposed improvements' to our local Common.

Now I for one don't believe the Common needs improving. It looks ghastly at the moment because the Gas Board has seen fit to lay a huge pipeline across it, and the place is swarming with bulldozers and lorries. But normally it consists of 70 acres of lovely open country, where dogs and children gambol, wild flowers bloom and the weary stretch out in the sunshine. However up-tight I'm feeling, an hour rambling along its grassy rides restores my good humour and equilibrium.

Now it appears that the Putney Society had set up a working party in January to see how the Common could be improved, and its draft report was to be discussed at the meeting. Disquieting rumours had also filtered through that 'improvements' were a euphemism for the Cricket Club's plot to grab a large section of the Common for a second cricket pitch. Convinced that one cricket pitch is enough, I decided to go along and see what the fuss was about.

A large crowd had gathered, including a militant band of dog-walkers, members of the Cricket Club, representatives from the Scouts, our next-door neighbour who has the cleanest car in Putney, a posse of vigorous lady botanists, a depressed-looking curate, and my husband and I, who were not speaking because he'd decided to support the new pitch.

In the chair was the Chairman of the Putney Society, Judge Ian Fife, a Gary Cooper figure, handsome, suntanned, with grey hair and a peremptory manner. 'You're going to hear a lot of my voice this evening,' he said, smiling like the Wolf in Red Riding Hood, 'but that's the way the cookie crumbles.'

Next moment the smile was wiped off his face as an even more handsome and authoritative man with grey hair stalked in and sat at the back.

'Who's that?' I whispered in excitement.

'The Ranger,' said my neighbour. 'He's in charge of the Common.'

Evidently the Ranger is employed by Putney and Wimbledon Conservators, a body of local dignitaries who control the Common, and who are quite separate from the Putney Society. I wondered if the Ranger would shoot it out with Judge Gary Cooper before the evening was out.

After a preamble on how the working party had been set up, which sent a bald man on my right to sleep, the judge turned to a map of the Common and took us on a laborious conducted tour. Pointing to the north sector, which is flanked by a deep brook, he said: 'We feel there is much room for improvement here, for more interesting trees and shrubs to give the area an appearance of natural beauty as on Barnes Common.'

This was red rag to a bull. There is great rivalry between the two commons, and although Putney may lack the rather stylised lushness of Barnes Common, no one who has seen the sun slanting on its newly mown hillocks, or the elms rising darkly out of the brook, could call it deficient in natural beauty.

The judge's stick passed over the lovely green stretch of grass rumoured to be the site of the second cricket pitch. 'Now this area,' he said with heavy cunning, 'could *never* become an area of natural beauty.'

He then moved on to the existing cricket pitch, becoming quite lyrical: 'And what better sight than a lot of people in white flannels playing cricket?'

'Speak for yourself,' hissed the dogwalkers.

Now he indicated the stretch of land next to the cricket pitch: 'Nor is there any facility for our young people to play football. A properly laid out football pitch for boys — and if necessary for girls,' he added hastily, 'is a reasonable thing.'

He then proceeded to stun the meeting by saying the working party intended turning the Common into a sports arena with not merely a new cricket pitch, but also two football pitches, a putting green and two 'kiddies' adventure playgrounds.

'There'll be balls everywhere,' thundered an old lady.

'Bloody Wembley,' said a dogwalker.

The Lone Ranger got to his feet — you could almost hear the strains of *William Tell* — and stalked out of the meeting in disgust. Probably aware there were factions about to lynch him, the judge called a break for coffee. Cabals then gathered in corners, muttering furiously.

After the interval, the fun became fast and furious. Different factions shooting down every idea proposed by the working party, rather on the principle of that *Punch* joke: 'Go and see what Baby's doing, and tell her she mustn't.'

'How can they be expected to plant interesting trees,' complained an earnest young man, 'when vine-dals are always pulling them up?'

'Young saplings,' said a lady botanist, 'were not helped by the countryman's natural instinct to slash as he goes along.'

A squawking match then developed because the cricket club wanted the bridle path which crossed the Common moved to accommodate more of the outfield of their existing pitch.

'Why don't you move the pitch?' bellowed an enraged commuter to loud cheers.

'We'll buy a goat and tether it on your wicket,' said a pretty mother, lobbying for the adventure playground.

An old lady got up and launched into a long story about how her hubby had passed away having a stroke on that very bridle path, and she didn't see why she had to pay

Common Rates now. The man with the bald head was still sleeping peacefully.

Now it was the turn of the residents of adjacent flats (appropriately called Common View) to start howling about noise from the proposed kiddies' adventure playground. A bright spark suggested putting the adventure playground near the brook, where it wouldn't disturb anyone.

'But surely the kiddies would drown in the brook?' said an anxious mother.

'Oh, not the sort of children we have in mind,' said the judge.

'Inflatable ones?' muttered a dogwalker.

I'm surprised they didn't suggest piranha fish in the brook to add to the adventure.

With feeling running really high, we moved on to the proposed cricket pitch. Someone asked why the Cricket Club needed another pitch. Because, he was told, the Social Club (which everyone else in Putney calls the 'Ut) was too far away from the present pitch, and it meant the little Colts had to cross dangerous roads to get to it.

'Why not move the 'Ut, then?' said a dogwalker.

'The reason they want another pitch near the 'Ut,' said a local stalwart, 'is they drink so much Red Barrel beforehand they don't like having to run across two main roads every time they go to the toilet.'

Rousing cheers all round. Everyone was shouting. The judge called for order and the tone was raised by a smoothie in a striped shirt from the Cricket Club, who spoke of the need for another pitch for the second eleven (funny when they only managed to field ten players that week) and of the vital part the Cricket Club plays in giving the Colts an interest and keeping them off the streets.

Dogwalkers at the back started sawing on imaginary violins.

Someone then asked the judge to show how far the proposed playgrounds and pitches would reach. To howls of derision he drew two minute football pitches and a cricket pitch so small any mouse could have hit a six on it.

'And there's plenty of room for a hockey pitch in the middle,' he added with a laugh.

The audience looked at him stonily.

'Let's get up a partition,' said an old lady.

'Let's have a vote,' said a dogwalker sensibly.

The judge said it was not the aim of the meeting to have a vote, but that the working party's proposals in an amended form would be put before the Conservators in the autumn.

'But how will they know the strength of the opposition unless we vote?'

The judge shrugged.

'So what was the point of us coming here at all?' said a man furiously.

'I really don't know,' sighed the judge.

The meeting broke up in uproar.

To the working party, which had obviously laboured long over the draft report, the reaction of the meeting must have seemed obstructive, ungrateful and even slightly hysterical. But until it is threatened, I don't think one has any idea how deeply protective, as a town dweller, one feels about one's commonland. Particularly today when more and more of the country round towns is being eaten up, and at this moment a huge crane hangs like a malignant bird of prey over the trees south of the Common, putting up another high-rise block to ruin the landscape, and box people in farther from 'the earth, the dear green earth.'

In these gloomy days, too, one has become infinitely caring about simple things — yarrow starry white along the pathway, the bright blue gleam of a jay's wings, squirrels gathering acorns — that quicken the heart but are not subject to inflation.

If the Conservators were to grant space for all these pitches, what's to stop lobbies next year for a race track, a rugger pitch and a kitten's adventure playground? It seems more important for people to have a stretch of unspoilt land where they can wander in peace, which is a word the do-gooders don't seem to understand.

Nativity plays

We all have our nativity play memories. My husband played Joseph once, a thrill somewhat blighted by the fact that the Blessed Virgin was played by a very plain boy called Bleesdale. And when my father was at Chatham he and two brother officers were approached by the admiral's wife to appear in a mystery play. Thinking it must be Edgar Wallace and all being rather smitten with the admiral's daughter, they agreed with alacrity, but alas ended up draped in curtains with the opening line: 'We be three shepherds from the hills.'

Leafing through our photograph drawer the other day I found a picture of my old school nativity play. There they all are — Sheena Duncan, the school beauty as the Angel Gabriel; Hannah Nixon blacked up as a king; Hilary Jepson, who first told me about Tampax, as the inn-keeper; Ann Lawson-Dick has since become a tycoon in the city; Rosie Langley, my best friend, whom my mother disapproved of because she had a Yorkshire accent and a mother who enjoyed gentlemen friends and gin-and-orange in the afternoons.

I myself can be seen kneeling at the front already typecast as a hedonistic tax-collector friend of the inn-keeper who repents at the end.

There we stand, an angelic group of nine-year-olds gazing at a doll in a manger of straw. But the ructions that took place behind the scenes would rival any Mia Farrow—Robert Redford vendetta on a Hollywood set.

'Girls, girls this is a religious play,' our headmistress would plead as she caught one of the Kings having a punch-up with the heavenly host, or surprised Joseph playing Jacks with the Oxen when he should have been making his entrance.

Cherubim and Seraphim cried continually too, because they were always being pinched by the shepherds, who resented having to wear beards.

There were also rows over the future of baby Jesus, a perfectly good doll who said Mama and closed her eyes when she lay down. I remember pleading my case: 'She'll be so lonely if you shut her up for a whole year in a beastly old dressing-up box.'

Entr'acte we sang carols, everyone coming in heavily on the Come Let us Adore Him, which we knew, but with the verses about abhorring the virgin's womb and the breastful of milk omitted in case they made someone giggle.

On the night, despite the star fusing and an angel dripping hot wax from her candle on to the Ass's backside, the performance went well. All the parents were in floods of tears, including my father. The left-hand bottom corner of the photograph even catches the back of his head sitting dutifully in the front row. He is a very tall man, and to his chagrin it was the first time any of us realised he was going bald.

But that was all long ago, and now my children are growing up I'm deep in the nativity swing again. 'You know the Virgin Mary,' said my son last week. 'She's Kevin's sister.'

Extraordinary pieces of information keep filtering through:

'You know old God, he's visible and lives up in the sky but he's got a heater, Jason White says so.'

Last week All Scents staged their play in the local church. It was the inevitable tearjerker, but things have got so sophisticated these days, with all the cast miming to taped songs from *Jesus Christ Superstar*, and the whole play videotaped by a handsome BBC cameraman whose wife supervises the school dinners.

Behind me a large woman was being determinedly good with her grandchild, pointing to the lovely Burne-Jones stained-glass windows. 'And in that one you can see Uncle David, and there's Uncle Pax, and there's Auntie Perpetua, and there at the end is Uncle Solomon who knows absolutely everything.'

'Everything?' said her grandson sceptically. 'Does he know if Fulham are going to beat West Brom on Saturday?' Rather like the catch phrase circulating All Scents at the moment:

'We three kings from Orient are. No we're not, we're from Chelsea.'

A host of angels rose up at the altar, their arms raised like President Nixon. The shepherds gathered round Mary and Joseph, one clutching a rabbit with blue ears. With all their middle-east headdresses, they looked rather like the private ward of a National Health Hospital.

'Jesus Christ Super Star,' pounded the tape recorder. Mary held up her baby in triumph like a newly-landed monster trout.

Later in a classroom we saw it all played back on video-tape. The film jerked a bit like Charlie Chaplin, but the camera picked up some interesting detail: the orchestra from Class Three very professionally shaking spit out of their recorders, the pretty blonde, choir mistress mouthing frantically behind a pillar, the first king wearing mountain-eering boots like Sherpa Tensing beneath his robe. There was my son's round grinning face in the congregation, and me in a huge sheepskin coat sobbing quietly into my hymn sheet.

But why was one crying? Because the whole thing was so enchanting? Or for one's lost innocence? Or for the dark future which seems at present to loom over both us and our children?

I think most of us would like to recapture the Christmas spirit, but find it difficult. I am reminded of Hardy's poem about the oxen, in which he says that as a child he believed totally that at midnight on Christmas Eve, the oxen kneel down in their pens to honour the birth of Christ.

Later when he grew old and disillusioned, he goes on

Yet I feel if someone said on Christmas Eve,
Come and see the Oxen kneel . . .
I should go with him into the gloom
Hoping it might be so.

At the wedding

Everyone told me how lucky I was to have a seat in the Abbey. But what, after all, was I going to see? A bridle couple, who among their numerous wedding presents had already received eighteen copies of the *Encylopaedia of the Horse*.

We had been soured, I suppose, by the glut of trivia and scraping of double-barrels in the Press over the last few weeks. Or by that dreadful television interview with its unctuous Stars on Sunday atmosphere. After all this ballyhoo, how could the wedding itself be anything but an anticlimax?

The omens, however, were good on the morning. Brightly dawned their wedding day.

Outside the Abbey, it was like the first day of the sales. All the Press had got there early in the hope of sneaking inside for some extra titbit — only to discover they weren't allowed in until 10 a.m.

It was bitterly cold. The flags swooned and rallied. Young Dragoon officers decked out in their finery of dark blue tunics, gold sashes, gleaming spurs and the tightest trousers stood around looking glamorous.

'I hope Mummy sees me on television,' said one beauty stroking his hair.

Big Ben chimed 10 a.m. and we all surged inside. The Abbey looked glorious. The perfect theatrical-set.

Everything: altar, carpets and chairs seemed to be in cherry pink or gold like a page out of the *Tailor of Gloucester*.

Down below guests were arriving. Sheila Sim and

Richard Attenborough, Dorian Williams and his wife like a pair of elegant greyhounds. One felt he should have been doing the commentary.

The women's fashions were conservative. Several beauties with good enough cheekbones got away with turbans. Members of the bi-plane set were out in force in mildewed furs, pull-on felts, no eye make-up, a good regimental panache.

A faint smell of veneration, mothballs and eau de cologne hung on the air.

Soldiers were everywhere. How shiny and well brushed upper-class men wear their hair! I suppose it's a hangover from Nanny and her 100 strokes a day.

The Phillips family was arriving now. I bet there was a general inspection beforehand in case anyone let the side down. But they all looked very respectable, hemlines on the knee, flared coats, lady mayoress hats.

Next came the foreign royals — talk about Abbey International. The Press was going spare trying to identify everyone. There's Norway. No it isn't, it's Sweden, no it isn't, it's Greece. A bit like Miss World — only this time it was the men who wore the sashes.

Behind me an American lady was driving an English journalist mad trying to identify everyone:

'Who's that?' she asked finally, as an ancient official shuffled past.

'That's Prince Nigel of Surrey,' he said evenly.

'Is that a fact, how do you spell that word Surrey?'

A rumble of interest swept the Abbey at the arrival of Princess Grace. I don't know why anyone objected to her wearing white. She looked almost matronly in her tent coat as she sank into her seat like a great swan. But what a beautiful woman she is, entirely untouched by time though not by Prince Rainier, who was carrying a black top hat, and looked like a 1930s movie star playing a waiter.

Then two magnificent plumed old military men, epaulettes gold jelly moulds, took up their positions on either side of the steps, for the royal family were now due any minute. First came Princess Alice in mauve, and she was shown to one of the uncomfortable pink seats.

'They might have given her a throne,' grumbled the American journalist, 'a gracious old lady like that.'

Then suddenly we were overwhelmed by a great flock of royals, like a bridge hand full of court cards. There was Alexandra in green velvet, looking like a sexy landgirl, Angus Ogilvy radiating solidarity. The Duchess of Kent shepherding two very blond children followed by the Duke of Kent, who looks, now he's balding, like a patrician Clement Freud. There was Princess Margaret, splendidly gaudy and flamboyant, the Prince of Wales, flushed and in good birthday spirits, and Richard of Gloucester, more like a chemistry student than a Prince.

But the one who held one's eyes was the Queen in brilliant sapphire blue and a hat with no hair showing — a hard style which emphasised how tense she looked, her eyes red as though she'd been crying all night.

The Queen Mother by comparison was so smiling and resplendent in gold and fur, she nearly outshone the lumbering armada of clergy in their glittering robes who followed the royals up to the altar.

We then had our first glimpse of Captain Phillips. He certainly looked beautiful in his scarlet tunic, and so endearingly true blue and straight, like a P.C. Wren hero. Next door Captain Grounds like a warm-up man fed him with a volley of jokes. But although Captain Phillips acted relaxed, one could see through borrowed binoculars the white of his knuckles as his hands clenched his sword.

Suddenly we all jumped at an ecstatic fanfare of trumpets and there was Princess Anne on the monitor arriving at the Abbey. Slim yet voluptuous and regal as well — a touch of Glenda Jackson playing the young Elizabeth. At 11.30 exactly, she started her long trek up the aisle. The organisation had been faultless. Marlborough himself couldn't have planned a campaign better. Prince Philip looking both proud and amused walked beside her, handsome as a smooth-haired Charlton Heston. After what seemed an unconscionable time, she drew level with Captain Phillips and they turned and smiled at each other.

Dearly Beloved, intoned the Dean of Westminster. No one could see any impediment why the couple shouldn't be joined. But such was the theatrical atmosphere, one half expected old sourpuss Willie Hamilton to shoot up through a trap-door in a puff of smoke. The Archbishop in his rose-embroidered robes beamed down on the couple.

Mark Anthony Peter, wilt thou have this woman to thy wedded wife?

We crossed our fingers, but his responses came out clipped and clear without the trace of a stammer. Then it was Anne's turn and her voice sounded high, more like her mother's than the nasal drawl she employs on telly.

The marriage service over, everyone relaxed. Anne and Mark went off to pray. The best man's trousers were so tight he had to come down the steps sideways. Prince Philip joined the Queen, who still looked unhappy. One felt she was suffering from a very human mixture of emotions — grief at losing a daughter, and nostalgia for her own wedding twenty-six years before.

'All weddings make one think of one's own wedding,' gushed a woman journalist.

'They make me think of all three of mine,' said William Hickey.

Princess Anne's Godfather was now asking God to make the Princess a follower of holy and godly matrons. One couldn't help thinking of those army wives waiting to ply her with plonk and curry.

Another fanfare and off they all went into the vestry. The television cameras roamed lasciviously over golden cherubs and the better-looking of the choir-boys. Back came the royals looking more cheerful. The organ broke into that Toccata which sounds as if the record's stuck, and down the aisle came Mr and Mrs Mark Phillips. How glamorous and carefree they looked now, as though they were galloping the final lap of honour with rosettes pinned to their bridles.

Out into the sunshine they went, and the bells rang out.

As one of the dragoons said later: 'It had the same sort of family atmosphere as my sister's wedding in the country.'

When I got home, thoroughly elated by the whole thing, my daily, who'd seen it on telly, was waxing lyrical: 'It was history wedded to the present. We've got nothing like it at all back in Ireland. If I live a hundred years I'll never see anything so lovely, and any Englishman who isn't proud of it ought to be shot.'

A slow wiltz at the Vienna ball

I was knocked out to be asked to the Vienna Opera Ball — 7,000 people, including the cream of European Society, waltzing the night away to the strains of Johann Strauss. Here at last was my chance to break into the Jet Set. Perhaps I might catch the eye of an archduke and be spirited away to a night of passion in a schloss.

I borrowed a gorgeous Gina Fratini dress, floating and pale blue and covered in upside-down fairies, and spent the week before practising my quick waltz in gum boots all over Putney Common. It was vital, I felt, to keep up with the Johanns.

Eine Kleine Nacht Musik poured out of a loudspeaker on the plane. Our party consisted of a relentlessly amiable public-relations man from the Austrian Tourist Board, a svelte blond from the *Scotsman*, a William Hickey reporter with a very grand voice who thanked everyone ver' ver' much for everything, a Hickey photographer and a loquacious Austrian lady called Gretel Bear, who the PR man said was 'Up' in Austrian Society. The Hickey man's eyes gleamed. He and Gretel Bear were soon nose-to-nose, sussing out the celebrities to come.

Lunch was delicious — good plane cooking. Mountains started appearing through the cloud like shepherd's pie when you haven't enough Smash to cover the mince. We landed in Vienna. And what a breath-taking city it is: golden palaces, ice-green domes, and cold clear air coming off the mountains. Each building seems to celebrate the rampant hedonism of the Viennese. On every ledge, pomegranates spill, leaves sprout, cherubs gambol, muscular

114

giants wrestle, and heraldic lions raise paws. You feel a worship of the Imperial past almost amounting to necrophilia.

I dressed in feverish excitement, but, waiting in the hotel foyer, soon realised gloomily that the competition for archdukes was going to be pretty hot. For all the women from 17 to 70 were absolutely stunning, tanned from ski-ing, their hair gleaming and dyed glorious colours, swatched in huge feather boas.

The men were equally glorious — big, blond, heel-clicking, and weighed down by sashes, stars and ribbons.

Our party assembled, increased now by a very tall Girl Guide from the Viennese tourist board called Traudl. Gretel Bear removed strands of ostrich feather from her scarlet lip, and pointed out who was related to whom to William Hickey.

'I wonder if Gretel's related to Rupert Bear,' said the *Express* photographer.

On to the ball. The Opera House blazed with light, but every entrance to the ballroom was blocked by an impenetrable phalanx of backs. On the platform men in gold capes raised trumpets to their lips. Large men pressed their medals into my bare back. I was suffering from Claustria-Phobia. Still, I could see the stage, where the band and 176 debs and their partners had gathered to open the ball. All in white, the debs wore coronets rather like the little lion in the Egg Board ads, and held bouquets of red roses in trembling white-gloved hands.

Then the band broke into a polonaise, and the girls and their partners poured down the stairs and disappeared behind a forest of backs, floating around, presumably, on the soft waves of the Blue Danube.

I couldn't see a bloody thing except the occasional flash of tulle, but it seemed a cross between *Come Dancing* and *Swan Lake* — more Ostrich Lake, really, when you looked at all the boas. Finally the conductor shouted *Waltz*, and the ball was open to everyone.

The Hickey Man, of course had seen it all: 'The most beautiful thing I've ever seen,' he said, 'but of course, I can't use it.' He then bore his photographer off into the mêlée to root out celebrities, which left the relentlessly amiable PR man to cater for Gretel Bear, Traudl, the girl from the *Scotsman* and me. Not that I have anything against my own sex, but four to one is not a happy ratio at a ball. Everyone else was firmly in parties. Even the most smouldering glance could not have extracted an archduke.

'This is one of the most exciting nights of my life,' said the PR man as he led Traudl off to dance. Gretel Bear was discussing boiled beef with the girl from the *Scotsman*. I wandered round. The opera house itself looked magical, lights like bunches of white grapes blazed from the ceiling, 140,000 carnations fell in coral pink waterfalls from the boxes, which cost £1,000 each to hire. Every one was packed with ravishing, chattering people, flirting and drinking champagne, their conversation full of exclamation marks, which sounded like the talking bits in *Fidelio*.

The vast ballroom was now entirely filled up with whirling couples — like one of those scenes on television from *War and Peace* or *The Pallisers*, when you say *Isn't it a pity people don't give parties like this today?*

Traudl went to the Ladies, the girl from the *Scotsman* disappeared. I finished up everyone's glasses of champagne, acutely conscious of being a Waltz flower. A handsome man shot me a hot glance and I rammed my elbows together to deepen my cleavage. He looked away. I felt as desirable as a pork chop in a synagogue. A nice American lady in a lot of grey chiffon sat down beside me, and said that this was her first stay in Vienna. 'My friend Lilian,' she added, 'has been enjoying strange foreign balls all month.'

Norman Mailer, she went on, had written the introduction to her last narvel. I wondered if I ought to ask her to dance.

De-dum, de-dum, de-dum, called the incessant beat of *Tales from the Vienna Woods*. The girl from the *Scotsman* returned. 'Half of them haven't shaved under their armpits,' she said. The consistently amiable PR man danced and danced, his little feet twinkling on the floor.

116

My upside-down fairies drooped. I would have been grateful now for a right-way-up fairy, he might at least have asked me to dance.

From a nearby looking glass, I saw my curls had all dropped out. Beside the glossy Viennese, I looked not unlike our shaggy English setter, when he came last in the local dog show. Although I pretended at the time I'd entered him just for fun, I felt the judges and the Viennese men ought to have seen through the shaggy exterior to the beautiful soul beneath.

Couples were waltzing now in every passage, while in the buffet the unloved found compensation in goulash soup. Elderly ladies eased swollen feet out of gold slippers. Rows and rows of chauffeurs waited wearily at the front door. I was ready for bed.

Back at our hotel, Gretel Bear, still talking, was eating Mozart Balls made of marzipan. In bed I played with the telephone, which was like a Fisher-Price toy, providing music on four stations, and with buttons to summon floor walkers, door openers and chamber maids. Better to be sloshed than schlossed.

Next morning, wandering round Vienna, we passed a shop called a House of Gentlemen. 'Pity they didn't sell us a couple for last night,' said the girl from the *Scotsman*.

When I got home to Putney, I was touched to see in our front garden that the first wallflower had come out in sympathy.

Housework

'I'm going to write about housework this week,' I said.

'But you never do any,' said my neighbour tartly.

Although somewhat crestfallen, I had to agree with her. I make a lot of noise in the kitchen sighing and banging saucepans, but most of my time is spent undoing housework done by other people. Between them they leave the house immaculate during the week, but on Saturday I take over and by Monday morning I have reduced the place to a shambles.

Matters are particularly bad at the moment, because with the repeated spells of mild weather the cats and the dogs are moulting all over the carpets three months early. With the recent rain too, the garden is like the Somme and every time the dogs come in they spread mud everywhere. Meanwhile the cats pour in through the cat door, and being wary of the dogs, they move around the room above floor level, leaving a tracery of black marks on the furniture and kitchen surfaces — which I try to look at with a painter's eye and fail. Many hands may make light work, many paws don't.

Added to this, the washing machine and the cleaner seem to be starting the change of life. The cleaner in particular refuses to pick up anything. Hardly a day passes without the driving band cutting its throat on a bit of shredded bone (the puppy again) and I always seem to rupture those cleaner bags. You force them on like condoms and end up in a cloud of dust.

But these are just excuses. I'm lousy about housework because I'm untidy and because I'm so easily sidetracked.

Sometimes I pretend the Queen — now perhaps it should be Mrs Thatcher — is coming to lunch in order to spur myself on to greater endeavour, launching into a flurry of cushion plumping.

Then I start wondering if my curtsy would pass muster and practise it in front of the mirror, and in two seconds I'm trying on lipstick.

Or take my progress, noted in horrified fascination by my husband last Sunday morning: At 9.30 am: give children Weetabix, scrub kitchen surfaces with Vim, children ask for toast, cut off crusts and have to clean surfaces again, stop to read old copy of *Horse and Hound*, clean sink, peel potatoes and dirty sink, remember animals haven't been fed, open tins, stop to read special offer on Pedigree Chum tin, feed animals, read article on Sir Keith Joseph on newspaper under cat's plate, clean surface and sink, admit guilt about the goldfish, dirty sink changing water, clean sink, then dirty again dunking moribund azaleas. Eat two pieces of toast with marmalade, using five knives and two spoons, sweep dust into a pile in the kitchen, stop to admire high rise block of Lego while collecting the dustpan and brush, by which time the junior dog has chased the senior cat through the pile of dust.

It is difficult to steer a middle course with housework. You read women's magazine articles about housework being a negation of life and how glad you'll be when you look back that you let the washing-up pile up that Wednesday so you could make doll's clothes for the children.

On the other hand as you gaze despairingly across a toy-strewn paw-trodden hall on Sunday night, you think of the Greek love of order and beauty. Or as I watch my husband knot his tie extra tightly to conceal the fact that the top button of his shirt is missing, I am reminded of the fact that behind every successful man there's a clockwork wife.

My real problem is guilt. I don't mind dirt *per se*, I certainly don't lose any sleep over the richer dust concealed on the top of the wardrobe, but I worry about other people thinking I'm a lousy housewife. It's the age-old preoccupation with appearances.

Keeping up with ultra-hygienic nannies, for example, has reduced me, and subsequently the entire family, to neurotic tatters in the past. About 4 p.m. on Sunday, I'd start panicking that the place wouldn't be spotless enough for her return on Monday morning. I'd begin frantically moving milk bottles from one side of the sink to the other, and scream at the children if they spilt Ribena on the floor.

The reason for all this introspection is a frightfully earnest book I've been reading this week called *The Sociology of Housework*, by Anne Oakley,* written in such convoluted prose that it's much harder work ploughing through it than cleaning 15 baths after a rugger team.

The author interviewed forty housewives and in order that they might remain anonymous called them different and very grand names like Elaine Cawthorne, Dorothy Underwood and Eleanor Driscoll. I must say I was rivetted by how much housework some of them seemed to do:

'I never sit down,' said a plasterer's wife called Marylyn Thornton.

Another woman said she did 105 hours housework a week. If Joe Gormley was her union leader she'd be on £12,000 a year. She washed her curtains, net and otherwise, once a fortnight, washed all the carpets once a week, spring-cleaned her bedroom every day, and always fed the three year-old child with a spoon because "she makes a mess if she feeds herself." Her husband, she went on, was seldom in — hardly surprising.

Another housewife said she always changed the sheets twice a week:

'Once the machine broke down, we had to go for eight days, we all felt dirty, everyone complained.'

The only housewife I felt remotely drawn to was one who read books all the time:

'I only do about ten minutes a day, I've got very low standards, I think housework's a waste of time.'

There are also lots of questionnaires and equations about husbands and whether they qualify as high, low or

*Published by Martin Robertson.

medium. I don't need equations to tell me that, when he comes in from the pub, my husband's high, when my friends come to stay he's medium, and when his bank statement arrives he's low.

But according to the book, he qualifies as an extremely good husband who pulls his weight, but not quite as good as the husband who washes clothes, washes up, puts the children to bed, and even presses his suits. My husband presses his suit — but not on an ironing board.

I love all the jargon too. The next time I say Hullo to my son, I'm indulging in 'child socialisation', and the next time my husband fails to help with the washing up, I can accuse him of 'over-conscious adherence to gender-role stereotype in the domestic area.'

The author keeps going on how degraded women feel saying I'm just a housewife at parties. In America to make it sound more creative, one says, 'I'm a home maker.'

But on the whole, the survey makes pretty good sense. According to the housewives interviewed, it appears that many women get immersed in housework, or 'domestic engineering' as it is now called, only to fill in the time between their husband's departure in the morning and his return from the pub in the evening.

I think women should do housework all day if they really get pleasure out of it, but as Christopher Fry once said:

'What's the point of a halo? It's only one more thing to keep clean.'

Oh I am such a Tory Lady

I am a Tory Lady. You can tell me by my uniform: petal hat crammed down on my crenellated hair, regimental brooch, and tweed skirt just over the knee so that when I sit on platforms, I feel decent.

I will always refer to the lower classes as 'them,' but do not consider myself snobby. I get on *awfully* well with my Mrs G who refers to me behind my back as 'bossy boots.' I would like to be a JP and give very long sentences in a ringing voice.

I am a Tory Lady. I will spend more time brandishing tins with slits in the top at street corners. I will get a bigger bottom so I can sit on even more committees. I will go shopping pulling a basket on wheels containing a copy of the *Daily Telegraph* and slightly imperfect goods to be returned. I will try to like my radical son-in-law, despite the horrid things he says about Mr Churchill, and the way he tosses lighted cigarette ends into my herbaceous border.

Oh I am a Tory Lady. Every night I pray for those less privileged than I, who did not go to public schools. I will eat myself insensible at charity luncheons for the starving. I will comb the local paper for mentions of my name, and then complain furiously if it is spelt wrong.

I will patronise the arts. I will go to the theatre if only for a good sleep. I will attend Glyndebourne and the parish church, but wish they had better tunes. I will hang on my wall paintings by real artists purchased at Harrods. I will watch to the end of the late night television play, so I can cry 'Filth' every five minutes and then ring up the BBC.

Oh, I am a Tory Lady. I always wear pearls. (Someone

122

at bridge hinted it was common not to have little knots between each pearl — I wonder if it is.) One of the reasons I'm such a dedicated Tory lady is because I'm not quite sure of myself socially. I must remember to say 'Orf'.

I will send a food parcel to my sister in Rhodesia and my daughter Caroline in Kensington. When I go to London to purchase more petal hats, I will only lunch in department stores, eating my way through all three courses of the set lunch because I've paid for them.

I am a Tory Lady. I will never mention, nor think about, sex, which is something my husband Hubert used to do to me a hundred years ago and nobody else. I will shift photographs of my children and grandchildren to the back and front of the piano depending on who is in favour.

I will grit my teeth as the nestegg Hubert worked so hard to accumulate dwindles to nothing. I will try to be more economical. I will only telephone my children long distance when Hubert is shopping at Sainsbury's. Instead of spending money on eau de Cologne, I will use up all those bottles of Brut for Men my Irish son-in-law always gives Hubert for Christmas, which Hubert never uses.

Poor Hubert had a good war but he has not been having a very good peace . . . General Walker offered him the Area Command of the Bournemouth division — and now he's like an old war-horse sniffing blood.

Oh I am a stern and unbending Tory Lady. I am a one-man private army. I will constantly ferret out wrongdoing. I will flush out flashers from the long grass.

I will stand rigid to the last note of God Save the Queen. From whom, I wonder. Tory ladies like me, I suppose.

Oh come all ye officious and gentlewomanly. I will take pleasure in de-heading roses. I will labour to bring back hanging and flogging because I do not understand the human condition. I will strongly support corporal punishment (because I've never liked the other ranks). Post Election omnia Tory Ladies tristes sunt.

Oh Monday Club is fair of face. I will try not to wake at four o'clock in the morning drawn taut with fear like a piano wire. What will happen when our money runs out?

What will be my fête when the Russians take over? I am not young and comely as I was once.

My four o'clocks are the most terrible in the world. But perhaps with an overdraft of about £5,000 million, Mr Wilson's are worse (serve him right, *beastly* little man).

This is not a happy time for those with fixed incomes and fixed ideas. Let us fight on the beaches — Hubert and I always fight like hell on Bournemouth beach when we take the grandchildren. We shall never surrender.

I am still a Tory Lady. Oh take me to my leader. Perhaps Joseph and Mary will guide us to the promised land. I also have a high regard for Geoffrey Ribbentrop and Herr Thatcher. I wish I liked Enoch Powell as much as I like his policies. I wish Mr Heath was a gentleman like Mr Roy Jenkins. I will try to think of Mr Benn as Viscount Stansgate.

Oh I am a Tory Lady. I will disapprove when my daughter Caroline and her Scottish young man, who smells of garlic, do not rise from their beds until lunch-time — when you've been awake since four o'clock, lunch-time seems like midnight. I will also grumble constantly that the young never answer letters, but if one of them does, I will write back return of post putting them once more in my debt.

I so hope Hubert keeps up our BUPA payments. We used to go to old Dr Faith on the scheme until Dr Mukerjee took over his practice. No, I'm not prejudiced, I just feel natives are happier in Africa or between the pages of the *National Geographic*.

Oh I am a Tory Lady. I will tirelessly forage for jumble. I will trundle my trolley through hospital wards pressing second-rate romantic novels on the dying. All my life I have been selfishly working for others. I believe in the Middle Class Association, which was conceived by the Holy Gorst. Oh it's all the fault of the unions who are in the play of the Communists.

I will assist the police with their inquiries, and even if there is no tomorrow I shall go on bottling up my emotions — and plums. If only Hurbert and I could talk to one another, but every morning we are divided by the Iron Curtain of the *Daily Telegraph*.

Oh I am a Tory Lady at four o'clock in the morning, as sleepless and afraid, I look into the cold autumn dawn. I'm so lonely . . . but hark, all is not lost . . . if I really strain my ears I can just detect the happy sounds of a far-distant teenage party. I must wake up Hubert at once so that he can ring up and complain about the noise. After all, he *is* area commander now. Sleep Walkers of the world unite.

In the party spirit

I'm always excited by the idea of a party — I love all the thrill of the sexual unknown, a room crammed with quarry, opportunity knocking.

I love all the tarting-up beforehand too. In my teens I remember reading with amazement that the Duchess of Rutland — then Deb of the Year — could dress for a ball in 45 minutes. It used to take me at least three hours. There was the feeling that if you neglected any part of the ritual — eyepads in a darkened room with ankles higher than one's head, Arpege splashed behind the knees — you wouldn't be rewarded with appropriate booty later. I was impressed that Forever Amber once spent three days getting ready for a party.

Perhaps because I took so much trouble in those days, parties seemed more fun: pretending one was nineteen when one was fifteen, playing sardines with married men in vast centrally refrigerated houses.

Or there were Oxford parties, bliss because men outnumbered women by six to one, and everyone brought bottles of different things and tipped them into a huge bowl. Later you were invariably sick, or fell flat over bicycles in the hall on the way out.

I'm glad to report Oxford parties haven't changed. I was at one this summer, and an undergraduate in a white robe glided over to me:

'I felt compelled to speak to you,' he said, 'because I so admire your workman's wrists.'

When you're young, of course, what matters most is to appear to be attracting men, dancing every dance and not being the only member of the same flat not to be asked out to dinner after a cocktail party.

Today when no one talks to me at parties, I try to assume my lady novelist's face: it is entirely by choice I am standing alone. I am studying for material in Chapter Six.

Parties are a bit boring at the moment anyway because no one can talk about anything but the crisis.

'Is your husband pruning?' asked a stockbroker. 'No he hates gardening,' I said, only realising afterwards that he meant cutting down on staff.

'We even thought of throwing an inflation party ourselves, getting everyone to bring a fiver, and then serving up gin and bitter lemmings.'

But I've never really liked giving parties as much as going to them. Occasionally I have fantasies about having a salon, and inviting brilliant minds to my Thursdays. Then I make lists which start off Bernard Levin and Michael Holroyd and never get much further.

I'm put off, I suppose, by those magazine features which rabbit on about the enjoyment of host and hostess being the key to every party's success. But how can you enjoy yourself when you haven't been able to have a bath because it's full of ice, and the one celebrity you used as bait to get all the amusing people to accept, suddenly rings up to say his grandmother's died, followed by all your spare men ringing up to say they've got 'flu. (People are always banging on about the 'salt' and 'sugar' shortage — it's nothing to the dearth of spare men in London.)

Once the party gets going, there's always a reproachful bore on the sidelines, the man you keep trying to feed into a laughing group, who promptly spew him out again like the Hoover rejecting a screw.

And, worried that everyone won't get enough to drink, I always give them too much which means couples insulting each other, and people ending up prostrate on the floor like the first day of the Somme.

From the guest's point of view, of course, it's much more fun if everyone behaves abominably — you can judge a good party by the number of people who telephone next day to apologise.

But one has to be very charming to get away with wild behaviour for long. One doctor I know (who had the most marvellous double bedside manner) always took the precaution of ordering flowers beforehand — to arrive with an abject note of apology on the hostess's doorstep the morning after. Then he could behave badly with complete impunity. Unfortunately on one occasion the florist got it wrong and the flowers plus apology arrived on the afternoon *before* the party.

I myself don't deliberately set out to behave badly, but being shy I always down too many drinks to get myself going, and then suddenly my wicked alter ego emerges and makes smouldering eyes at happily attached men, and I cannon off groups like a shiny red billiard ball. Sober I'm very respectable but in Vino very tarty.

Mind you, one doesn't get much opportunity to behave badly at parties. As soon as a really attractive man starts seriously chatting you up, the hostess notices and charges over saying, she must break you up — like a French loaf.

Or every time you're furtively reaching the third digit of your telephone number, you're interrupted by the hostess's children, in bows and long dresses for the occasion, orbiting with the cashew nuts.

Magazines are always advising you to take trouble to talk to frumps at parties — 'you never know, she might have a fascinating brother' — and to boring men 'because if a handsome man sees you being vivacious, he'll think what fun you look and come over and talk.'

All that happens in my experience is the hostess thinks thank God someone finds old Blenkinsop amusing, and leaves you to it. And although I'm guilty myself, I hate hostesses who brandish any minor celebrity they've got hold of, committing one to desperately boring conversations with unknown pop stars, then adding defensively afterwards: 'Well, he's awfully big in Amsterdam.'

Or take a friend who went to a party given by a pushy lady in Majorca. During the evening there were fireworks. My friend sat down to watch them on one of the row of gold

128

chairs on the terrace. Instantly a waiter tapped him on the shoulder.

'You can't sit there, sir, these chairs are reserved for the Personalities.'

I note, too, with regret, that parties are getting noisier. I've been to two recently where there was no dancing but the music was so loud I couldn't hear a word anyone said. You can't go on saying 'What?' indefinitely. The only answer is to watch their teeth and roar with laughter when they do.

Another party I went to last week was full of the Beautiful People, eyes swivelling all the time, earmarking duchesses. And I always feel people are looking at my clothes and thinking 'not properly finished.' Rather like a friend of mine who went to a Beautiful Orgy in New York, and, finding, the hostess's bed covered in minks, said timidly: 'Do you take cloth coats, too?'

I wish I had the style of one splendidly eccentric old lady — alas recently dead — who, once when she had nothing to wear to a very grand party, cut a hole in the middle of a lace table cloth and wore it like a poncho over a body stocking. When, on arrival, the guests commented on it in stunned amazement, she simply raised it to shoulder level and said:

'Yes, and it seats eight, darling.'

Red under the bed

When it comes to politics, I always believe the last person I talk to. There was a shaming incident at the last election in which every canvasser who knocked on my door was so persuasive or good looking, that I promised each in turn that they could rely on my vote.

Come the election — I swanned into the polling booth to be faced by all three canvassers.

'There's Jill Cooper,' said a young man sporting a blue rosette, 'she's one of ours.'

'No she's not,' said a Socialist lady, consulting her notes, 'she's ours.'

'No, she's mine,' said the Liberal firmly. Crimson with embarrassment, I slunk into the night.

Overlaying such a flexible attitude, however, is a healthy distrust of Communism, so it was with trepidation I approached the TUC conference. I imagined it full of men with lean ascetic faces and threadbare suits, burning with hard gem-like flames and peddling their Marxist wares over cooling cups of tea.

My first intimation that I was wrong came in the train to Brighton. The first-class carriages were packed. The second-class virtually empty. Inside the conference hall sat rows of well-fed men, puffing cigars and displaying acres of sock.

On the platform backed by oyster curtains and flanked by two flower arrangements that would make Constance Spry turn in her compost, sat the TUC General Council. There was Flying Kite Tom Jackson, Jack Jones, like a scrubbed vicar, Len Murray with his well-pressed hair,

130

Richard Briginshaw, pink-faced and quiffed like an ageing D'Oyly Carte actor, Joe Gormley like a dissipated Ernie Wise, and Sidney Greene, looking boringly like himself, Vic Feather asleep in the gallery, and Hugh Scanlon (Hughie Red as opposed to Hughie Green).

I ploughed through the pile of literature I'd been given on arrival, and unearthed some bizarre unions. The Felt Hatters, who sound more like Tory ladies, and the Society of Wire Drawers — I wonder if they make chastity belts?

For the afternoon sessions, everyone looked even more flushed and convivial. If you'd lit a match, a great blue flame would have gone up from the brandy fumes.

Composite motion, as it was so charmingly called, followed composite motion. All afternoon rolled on the interminable periods of trade union oratory: let us not cross bridges before they eventuate, let us commence and take cognisance. The seats grew harder and harder.

'Up the Glottle,' wrote the man from the *New Statesman*.

'The Riot Act was read to union rebels today,' wrote the man from *Labour Weekly*.

'Dear Mother,' wrote the man from the *Daily Telegraph*.

All the action seemed to be going on in the passages outside where little knots of influential people gathered in corners whispering and conspiring.

On to a good party of Clive Jenkins — he grows more like Wilder in *The Power Game* every day. Although there was not enough tonic in the gin, or enough people to fill a very large room, everyone was very friendly — chips at the TUC Conference are eaten rather than worn on the shoulder.

A night of heavy parties followed with most of the delegates very much the worse for wear the next morning. The miners in particular looked as though acid indigestion was about to Industriously Act any moment.

Jack Jones kicked off with a rousing speech about pensions. 'Wasn't it wonderful,' I said afterwards, moved to tears.

'Wonderful,' said a fellow journalist, 'it's so good, he makes it every year.'

Whenever a do-gooder mounted the rostrum to dole out idealistic sincerity, the hall emptied and the tea room next door filled up. Delegates' wives wore Marks and Spencer sweaters so new they still had the creases in.

Lunch with Tom Jackson, surely the nicest man at the conference, restored my faith in human nature. As he smoothed his huge moustache before tucking into half a dozen oysters, I couldn't help thinking irreverently of the Walrus and the Carpenter.

Back at the conference, I had not only missed a glitteringly meretricious attack on the Lords by Clive Jenkins, but also a heckler during Jim Callaghan's speech.

It's always the same, you've only got to look the other way, and a wicket falls.

Jim was in the process of winding up; good rousing stuff. The moving finger jabs, and having jabbed goes on jabbing. I can never really take Jim seriously. He's too smooth, like a Galaxy milk chocolate commercial.

Later I was introduced to the newly elected Communist member of the General Council, Ken Gill, and here's one red one would not mind having in the bed. Extremely good looking, blazing with self-confidence, tall, broad-shouldered, with burnished curls and blue eyes carefully chosen to match his blue jacket. He would make the ideal Jack Tanner in *Man and Superman*, or a very good candidate for the Gatefold of *Cosmopolitan*.

Finally I spent the evening with the other Big Bad Wolf of the capitalist world, miner Mick McGahey. He has a ravaged sensitive face, not unlike Auden's younger brother. His voice saws hypnotically, punctuated by explosions of wild laughter, which crease his face into a thousand lines.

Nervous he might tear me to shreds, I was reassured when he gazed into my eyes, and promptly ripped off his glasses, revving up for the chat up. Here at last was the burning passion, the wintry dedication one had been waiting for. Whether he is talking about his deprived childhood

132

or how the tears streamed down his face when his pit pony was crushed to death, he is a spellbinder.

In fact one is so impressed by the affection beaming out of one eye, one rather misses the calculation shining out of the other.

He was also extremely irritated at a story put out by the Tory Press that he and Gormley had been gorging themselves on caviare on Sunday night.

'I've only had caviare once in my life,' he said, 'it was offered me in Moscow. Not knowing what it was, I said: "No thanks. I don't like bramble jam".'

The taxi driver who took me home said he had just brought Scanlon and Gormley back from Radio Brighton.

'Were they discussing burning issues?' I asked eagerly.

'No,' he said, 'they were grumbling because they hadn't been given enough time, because most of the programme had been devoted to Enoch Powell.'

Of books and bookmen

One of my weaknesses when I've had slightly too jolly a lunch is tottering out of Soho, along Piccadilly to Hatchards bookshop. Bibulous, I become bibliomaniac — and, not content with acquiring at least half a dozen books on the flimsy excuse that I might need them for research, I then feel guilty about the rest of my family and charge round the shop spending fortunes on children's books and military history. Thank God the cats and dogs can't read.

Hatchards, established nearly 180 years ago, is run by two whizz-grownups, very appropriately named Joy and Giddy. Tommy Joy, a pint-sized Dickensian optimist (office motto — the best is only *just* good enough for my staff) is the overall boss. Peter Giddy, Runyonesque and deadpan, buys in the books, and runs the shop. Since they took over ten years ago, they have boosted the turnover from £300,000 to much more than £1 million.

Last week I spent a day working in the shop trying to find out the secret of the book-selling trade. Putting on a bright Anyone for Tennyson smile, I lined up behind the cash desk with Peter Giddy, two pretty assistants, and a jolly Junoesque lady called Miss Parker who seems to know who wrote and published every book since the year dot.

Off we went ramming books into black and gold carrier bags, ringing up large sums on the till. *Among the Elephants*, lavishly displayed in the window, was selling well, so were the latest revelations about Dorothy Sayers. Outside the shop a disabled ex-serviceman was playing the

Waltz from Doctor Zhivago on the accordion. All the assistants wore flat shoes . . . I could see why after half an hour, my feet were killing me.

A woman strode in wearing a pull-on felt and a tweed coat. '*Ghosts of London*?' she brayed.

'You'll find them at the back of the shop,' said Miss Parker. Chauffeurs leaving their Rolls outside kept coming in to pick up books. A notice pinned to the cash desk said that Princess Maria of Jahore was waiting for the Cunards and Niarchos.

An old man with a monocle stood in the centre of the shop for an hour turning purple in the face as he read Leslie Thomas's *Tropic of Ruislip*.

'In one shop I worked,' said Peter Giddy, 'a man came in every day in his lunch hour and read *War and Peace*, and when he finished the manager gave him the book.'

I was staggered how hard the assistants worked, not just ringing up the till and putting pound notes under the bulldog clip, but the endless searching for books, and looking up in large works of reference to see if a book was still in print, then telephoning the publishers to see if it was available, and being charming all the time. Mr Joy went out beaming to lunch.

'Every day's like Christmas at Hatchards,' he said.

A middle-aged woman in a rust trilby was buying the Dorothy Sayers biography.

'A bit of a bombshell, wasn't it,' she said, 'I never knew she had a baby, but I shall still like her.' She added, turning rather pink, 'Isn't it mingy — the price of books today.'

Throughout the day we watched authors coming in and looking round the shop for their books, then surreptitiously sliding them up to the top of the pile.

A grey-haired assistant went out carrying a string bag: 'Do you think James is safe left in Natural History?' she asked.

During the lunch hour the shop filled up with brandy fumes, cigar smoke and striped-shirted smoothies from the clubs. Flat-sharers in headscarves, and students in blanket coats headed for the paperback department.

There were also hordes of Tory Ladies up from the country on whistle-stop tours taking in Harrods for a few remnants, breadcrumbed plaice, and sherry in the ladies' annexe, and the Turner Exhibition.

'Have you got *Quilting* by Margaret Cutbush?' shouted one.

The man on the accordion switched to Mighty like a Rose.

'Quick,' said Peter Giddy, 'put in a gardening window.'

'What ruderies have we got from W.H. Allen?' said Miss Parker, unpacking a large parcel of books. 'Dogs and Lions on the first floor,' she added in answer to a passing Deb.

People kept sidling up to me, and saying: 'Are you the Cash Desk?'

I nearly gave a young man a heart attack ringing up £20.75 for a novel costing £2.75, then nearly had a heart attack myself at the sight of my old dormitory prefect in a camel-hair coat and a green Alice Band peering at the Elephant book.

All I had to say was: 'Gosh, Piggy, do you remember me?' Instead, shaking with Upper Fourth nerves, I sneaked off to lunch. When I got back I learned that she'd bought three books, and I'd missed the Duke of Kent and John Le Carré.

I had a look round the shop.

One of the joys of the Rare Books department upstairs is that for 32p they will try to trace any book for you. Recently I was distraught to lose my copy of *Diary of a Provincial Lady* — within four weeks they had found me a first edition.

Next door, ablaze with colour, was the new children's book department, where it was nice to see old favourites like Little Black Sambo and Strewell Peter holding their own against Richard Scarry and Dr Seuss.

Rather too adjacent in the poetry department, two men in fur coats with handbags were noisily reading Baron Corvo's poems:

'Dear little boy whose bright brave face will so long o'er me lie,' said one.

'Let's buy it for Matthew,' said the other.

I went back to sell behind the cash desk. A man in a dirty mac strode up to me, breathing heavily. 'Where can I find crime?' he asked.

Two more Tory Ladies, scarlet from the hairdresser's, came in and read through the index of the Edward VIII book to see if they or any of their friends were mentioned.

Christopher Lee of Dracula fame headed for the history department sucking a sweet.

'Better than blood,' I said.

'Perhaps he's trying to give it up,' said Miss Parker.

A dramatic-looking man in a green cloak walked round the shop ostentatiously holding two copies of *Greenmantle*.

Down in the paperback department, a husband and wife were having tightlipped altercations over a Simon Raven novel.

'I know we haven't read it, Charles.'

'Yes, we have, Pamela.'

'We're always having that kind of argument down here,' said an assistant in an undertone. 'Paperback publishers change their jackets so often people never know if they've read a book or not.'

Nigel Nicolson's exposé of his parents' sexual junketings, now issued in paperback, was selling as well as the Elephants and Dorothy Sayers upstairs.

Obviously, if one wanted to produce a real blockbuster, one should encourage a literary Lesbian Elephant to write her memoirs.

The shop was closing, the lights being flicked on and off, and the last customers hurried out, as a glorious-looking blonde smothered in furs and Fortnum's carrier bags, with the air of one never refused admittance anywhere, sailed into the shop and bought a couple of novels.

'Too pricey for me,' said a male assistant looking at her wistfully, 'I'll have to wait until she comes out in paperback.'

137

Hunting with the hounds

I've always felt slightly guilty about being pro-foxhunting, so I decided last week to see the other side, and spent a day out with the antifoxhunting fraternity, or Hunt Saboteurs as they prefer to be called.

Two amiable earnest young men with beards and anoraks, a zoology student called Mike and an accountant called Iain, drove me down from London. Iain's girlfriend, a secretary, sat in the back. As a result of their propaganda on the way down I began to feel hunting was very wicked indeed:

'But Jill,' said Iain, 'only five per cent of foxes ever taste chicken.'

I had visions of them sitting down to coq au vin with a knife and fork.

Our quarry for the day was a Sussex pack called the Chiddingfold Farmers. Our rendezvous, the Noah's Ark pub in Lurgashal, one of those sleepy Stanley Spencer villages with a triangular green, red cottages edged by shaven yew trees, and a churchyard full of daffodils.

On arrival we exchanged firm handshakes and straight glances with other bearded Saboteurs. I was given a badge to wear saying Hounds off our Wildlife, and an aerosol can of Anti-Mate to spray on hounds and likely-looking huntsmen.

The Saboteurs had evidently been up half the night unblocking earths and spraying the area with aniseed. 'Sometimes we wave banners saying: "Only rotters hunt otters," ' said a pink-faced girl.

Several magenta-faced colonels and braying ladies on

shooting-sticks were giving us dirty looks. Labradors knowingly sat behind the grilles of shooting brakes as though they were about to take confession. A group of men in deer-stalkers and dung-coloured clothes stood grimly beside a Land-Rover.

'Those are the heavies,' whispered Mike. 'They're paid by the hunt to sabotage us.'

They looked very heavy indeed. I was beginning to feel uneasy, when suddenly hounds arrived, tails wagging merrily, and the hunt clattered off in its glory of scarlet coats, top hats and burnished horses.

Few sights can lift the spirit more. I decided one must remain loyal to one's prejudices and surreptitiously removed the Hounds off our Wildlife badge from my coat. Several Antis surged forward spraying the hounds with Anti-Mate.

'Keep your eyes peeled for foxes,' hissed the Chief Saboteur.

Hounds were put into a pale-green larch covert. We parked on the edge of a field above them, and next moment a posse of Saboteurs leapt over the fence, and armed with Anti-Mate, raced across the field, disappearing into the covert.

Immediately one of the heavies, his bottom vast in sage-green plus fours, pounded after them.

'If you spray any of that stoof,' he shouted, 'you'll get thoomped.'

On the other side of the trees, the top hats of the riders moved ceaselessly; upper-class voices drifted over the gorse towards us. Another posse of Saboteurs moved in from the right, view hallooing suddenly to distract the hounds and letting off two firecrackers which set all the horses plunging.

Pa pa pa pa pa came the tender melancholy note of the horn. 'Oh goodee, I mean, oh dear,' I said hastily, 'they appear to have found a fox'.

'That's Iain,' said his girlfriend proudly. 'He's learnt how to blow the horn as well as any whipper-in.'

A group of hunt supporters were looking at our car

threateningly. A bearded man in a beret with burning eyes leaned out of a passing Volkswagen: 'Are you an Anti?' he said in a low voice. I shook my head, resisting the temptation to say: 'Yes, I have four nieces and two nephews.'

A fat lady on a grey horse was having a squawking match with a group of Saboteurs.

'That's private property,' she said.

The Saboteurs laughed contemptuously like politicians in the House.

'Get off that horse, madam,' they said, 'and give it a rest.'

'This horse,' said the fat lady going pink, 'has more sense than you lot put together.'

Judging from the effing and blinding and shaking fists among the hunt servants, the Saboteurs had caused havoc in the covert. The Master decided to move on.

'Out of my way,' he said bossily to a group of girl riders. 'You're not with the pony club now.'

A lady supporter in a pull-on felt smoothed a wildlife park sticker incongruously adorning her windscreen, then gave an enraged bellow, as Mike and Iain, spattered with mud, their hands cut and bleeding from the undergrowth, tore up the hill, the heavies hot on their trail. They crashed through the hedge.

'Mind that fence, you absolutely bloody people!' she roared. Into the car they jumped and off we raced down country lanes, brushing the primroses on the banks, stopping from time to time to view halloo.

'We always leave girls to guard the cars,' said Iain, drawing up on the edge of a beechwood. 'Hunting people are still chivalrous towards women. If one of them tries to break our hunting horns, the girls shove them down their jerseys, and they won't touch them.'

I was beginning to feel sulky, I didn't want a horn up my jumper, I wanted to see hounds in full cry. Iain and Mike stood on a fence blowing a horn concerto, to the amazement of a flock of sheep who bleated back, a sort of Hallo-Ewe-There Chorus.

Finally we found hounds again in full cry inside the high

walls of the Petworth estate. Unable to get at them physically, the Saboteurs launched their toughest offensive. All hell broke loose, as smoke bombs and thunder flashes exploded, foghorns wailed, horns and whistles were blown.

I hid under a holly bush praying. The Saboteurs charged about yelling, screaming, encouraging, slipping on wet leaves, tripping over the long silver roots of the beech trees.

Hounds had evidently gone to pieces — all we could hear from the other side was whimpering, furious bellows and a lively stream of expletives. A Saboteur shinned up the wall to look. 'The Master's lost control,' he crowed, then clambered down hastily as a huntsman's face appeared over the other side, blazingly angry:

'I killed twenty Germans in the last war,' he bellowed, 'and all of them were more of a man than you lot.'

To the left, the Land-Rovers were moved up threateningly. The Saboteurs skittled back into their cars and, relentless to the last, roared round the Petworth estate trying to break in, but found each entrance blocked by supporters.

'Look,' said a heavy walking over to us, 'why don't you go home? You've completely wrecked our day.' I must say I agreed with him. The Saboteurs seemed to have a marvellous time, playing cops and robbers, spoiling everyone's fun, and feeling virtuous to boot.

As a hunting acquaintance said the other day: 'If they ever abolish hunting, I shall definitely become an Anti.'

Decadence

Decadence! What a delectable subject to write about — excess and exhaustion, and the worm i' the bud, and Dorian Grey, and those pale, cruel, sexually equivocal narcissists in the Tonik Ads.

But when I came to examine the word, I found it difficult to pin down. The dictionary defines decadent as 'decaying, degenerate, lacking in moral and physical vigour.' But most people today use the word to describe someone who is up to no good in a rather cool, stylish way.

When a woman calls a man decadent it usually means she thinks he's sexy — mad, bad and dangerous to know, in fact. But describing a *woman* as decadent is not nearly so flattering. I think of Norma Levy and poor Misses A, B and C dressed up in rompers and brandishing teddy bears in front of two-way mirrors and Kit-e-Kat producers. Goodness knows what they'll be up to by the time they reach the end of the alphabet.

I feel fantastically decadent if I go to the cinema in the morning, or to a drinking club in the afternoon, or read a novel any time at all during the day.

Equally I still feel a terrible shiver of guilt if I do a jigsaw puzzle and look at the picture, or play the pianola instead of the piano, or go up a mountain by cable car instead of climbing.

Decadent people grow their little finger nails extra long, wear lemon-yellow gloves, get up and go to bed late, and draw their bedroom curtains during the day. They also wear dark glasses all the time, and go out shopping in a fur coat and nothing else (this of course is permissible for dogs).

A friend of mine suggested the ultimate in decadence was getting an arthritic servant to iron your drawers. And I think one of the most decadent remarks was made by a divorce lawyer whose client couldn't think of any girls with whom he'd committed adultery.

'We'll make someone up,' said the lawyer, 'or the judge'll think you're a drip.'

Decadence of course is a word frequently applied to members of the upper classes — chinless wonders — the result of generations of in-breeding. I, being conceived in an hotel, am the result of Inn-breeding, but I'm much too middle class ever to be really decadent. My eyelids aren't heavy enough, and I blush too easily, and my legs are too short. You can't be decadent with short legs.

It's not, however, difficult to make rooms decadent. You paint them black or mauve, dim the lights, fill the place with monstrous fleshy tropical plants, and litter cushions about, instead of chairs. Sade went even better and used naked girls instead of furniture — much more interesting than stripped pine, and no one gets splinters.

It's only decadent to beat your wife if she starts enjoying it. It's decadent for a homosexual to marry a heterosexual just for appearances' sake. But I think the height of decadence was achieved by the man who was in bed with his mistress when his wife rang from the airport to say she'd arrived home a day early. Having kicked out his mistress, the man solemnly took the sheets off the bed, ironed them — and put them back again.

On the whole the English are very bad at being decadent. It's a pity we can't get it on the National Health — free issues of green nail polish and Spanish champagne. The French are much more adept, of course. Verlaine and Rimbaud's life together was an absolute pantomime of decadence, and Verlaine has given us the best definition:

'I love the word decadent,' he wrote, 'all shimmering in purple and gold, it suggests the subtle thoughts of ultimate civilisations, a high literary culture, a soul capable of intense pleasure . . . It is redolent of the rouge of courtesans, the games of the circus, the panting of the gladiator,

143

the spring of wild beasts, the consuming in the flames of races exhausted by their capacity for sensation as the trump of an invading army sounds.'

Rather like the King's Road, in fact. A dictionary might jib at Verlaine's definition, but one can see how it appealed to writers of the nineteenth century, when decadence became an accepted literary genre — Montesquieu inlaying the shell of his tortoise with turquoises of which the poor thing subsequently died, and Swinburne's friend Simeon Solomon submitting paintings of spiritual saintly beings to the Academy — painting the haloes round their private parts instead of their heads.

But I think that our whole attitude to decadence is quite illogical. Why is it considered decadent and a security risk for a Minister of the Crown to smoke pot, but quite acceptable if he gets sozzled every night on alcohol?

I also think any restriction on the right of free speech is decadent. I quite agreed with Richard Crossman over the Huntington affair, when he attacked those seventeen sycophantic Sussex University professors for supporting the mob action by the students which prevented Professor Samuel Huntington of Harvard from giving his lecture.

In fact most restriction of freedom is decadent. The Festival of Light telling me what I can watch on telly, and those birth control people telling me how many children to have, and all those whistle-blowing, watch-dogging Consumerists who quite happily enjoy all the advantages of the Affluent Society, yet spend their time clucking about it.

The problem with the word decadence is that it is used in two distinct ways — the first, when it describes something you think is rather dashingly wicked, the second pejoratively, when it is used to describe something you morally disapprove of.

My most trendy teenage friend tells me that to call someone decadent is the biggest compliment you can pay them. What did she mean by the word, I asked. She said she didn't know, but David Bowie was decadent.

Certainly the more sexy actors today have more than a dash of decadence and sexual ambiguity about them.

Malcolm Macdowell, Helmut Berger and Edward Fox, or in the older, more expensive age bracket, Alan Badel, Charles Gray and Alain Delon.

But whatever you feel about decadence, it ceases, like pornography, to be offensive when it is allied to wit. I think of Oscar Wilde and Noël Coward, and finally the sublime Tallulah Bankhead at that famous wedding watching the couple coming down the aisle, and turning to her neighbour saying in a loud aside, 'I've had them both and they were lousy.'

A bisexual made for two.

My measly excuses

Nothing tears me apart more than the conflicting loyalties of work and family. Take last week, for example. The school holidays were drawing to a close, my daughter was due back at nursery school on Monday, my son was going to a new school on Tuesday. We had had four non-stop weeks of visitors — great fun, but not conducive to work. Next week, I thought longingly, I'll get back to the typewriters and catch up.

Then two days before she was due back, in the middle of Sainsbury's at that point of no return, with a long queue behind and a pyramid of impulse buys on the cash desk in front, my daughter announced she felt sick, and engagingly spat Trebor Refreshers all over me. Next day she'd developed high fever, and the doctor diagnosed measles.

'Oh poor little duck,' I thought — then, in the next second: 'Oh God, bang goes another week's work!'

I raced as always for Mrs Beeton.

'Complications,' I read out, 'include bronchitis, pneumonia. An attack of mumps occasionally follows. Convulsions at the end can be fatal.'

'Oh, poor darling,' I said, 'she'll need her mother. But when the hell am I going to get all that work done?'

'Rubbish,' said my husband. 'The Nanny can look after her perfectly well. Measles is no worse than a bad cold these days.' And he promptly escaped to his office. But there are times even when you know someone else can look after your child perfectly well, that you feel bound to look after her yourself.

The first day my daughter was really ill. And, at the risk

146

of sounding soppy, nothing is more heartrending than a flushed haggard little face on the pillow, a hot hand clutching yours. Never do you feel more indispensable — for the first day at least.

Day two was another matter.

My daughter abandoned her Dame-aux-Camélias act, and emerged a scarlet-faced mini-Hitler, querulously screeching out orders like an Eartha Kitt played at 78.

'Read,' she kept howling, 'read NOW.' Then two minutes later: 'WANT a drINK!' and the incessant 'Turn OVER,' as every twenty seconds she got bored with the programme on TV. After an hour or two, my Florence Nightingale act was slipping badly.

I retired downstairs for a break. Ten seconds later she shrieked as though she'd been murdered. Racing up two flights, I discovered she'd lain on a cold flannel. I went downstairs again — another shriek. She wanted a biscuit. Finally she dropped off to sleep, and I grabbed an opportunity to work. But five minutes later there were more yells — she wanted to go to a birthday party. Deciding she must be delirious, and needed humouring, I let her put on her red party dress, which matched her face. She lay in bed raging with temperature like a stricken masquerader.

The doctor arrived with a pretty Scottish nurse.

'I'm terribly worried about her,' I said.

But upstairs, my daughter had made a dramatic recovery and, back in her nightie, all smiles, cheeks bulging with toast and jam, was watching a war film on TV. The senior dog rose and goosed the Scottish nurse, who said he was a tremendous 'pairsonality'. A religious programme followed the war film. The camera panned in on Christ on the cross. 'That's Jesus,' I said. 'He takes care of you.'

'No, he don't,' said my daughter. 'My Nanny do.'

She was plainly better. I shut myself away to work, but to no avail, for my worries had promptly shifted to my son and his first day at school the next day. His new-niform (as he called it) was already laid out — all unworn like a bride's.

147

I had also been worrying all the holidays about the fact that he couldn't tie his laces. We'd got round it until now by buying slip-on shoes, but the school's list specified lace-up gym shoes. I decided to give him a crash course, and bent over him, instructing, cajoling.

'Oy can't do it,' he said crossly, 'while Oy can hear you breathing.' Two minutes later I was presented with a perfectly tied bow. I felt as though I'd conquered Everest.

Euphoria evaporated with the arrival of my husband, who pointed out quite kindly that the char had dusted all the wires out of the hi-fi, that I'd forgotten yet again to collect his Grand National winnings from the betting shop, and that I was making too much fuss about my son's first day.

'How's Emily?' he said.

'Fine,' I replied sulkily.

'I told you measles was no worse than a bad cold.'

I slept badly that night, waking up every five minutes panicking that I wouldn't wake up in time to take my son to school. At 6.15, however, he wandered in bug-eyed but completely dressed in new uniform, collar askew, garters inside his socks.

'Did you sleep?' said my husband, when he woke up.

'Yes,' I lied, trying to be brave.

'I didn't — at all,' he said.

Later I took my son, wild with excitement, to school. His watchword, like Huckleberry Finn's, has always been 'trust in the unexpected.' He looked so vulnerable, disappearing into a sea of other blue-blazered boys. I drove home with a lump in my throat.

At least with him at school, and my daughter recovering fast, I felt I should get some work done. Total disaster. I couldn't settle to anything, fretting all day whether he'd be all right, would he like them, more important — would they like him?

Hours early, I tarted myself up and set out to collect him. I sat in the sunshine outside the school, biting my nails, watching elegant mothers drive up in their dark glasses and smart cars. Eventually, small boys appeared blowing down

148

rolled-up pictures, duelling with cricket stumps. I'll be good for ever, I prayed, if he comes out happy. The fore-court was now full of grinning pupils with pudding basin haircuts. Suddenly I recognised one of them as my son, not a tearstain in sight.

Information about his day filtered through on the way home — sporadically, like the first results on election night.

'We had fish fingers for lunch . . . and tadpoles, we did them in class. Oy asked a boy if he could do laces, he said No. Oy said Oy could . . . mostly. Oy've got a friend, but he was told to be because Oy'm a new boy. Moy friend doesn't wear gutters on his socks.'

Relief and joy flooded me. What on earth was the point of worrying about anything? Trust in the unexpected. Then, inevitably, came the sunset touch. My son eyed me beadily.

'Oy think,' he said, 'you ought to wear smarter trousers when you pick me up.'

Bedding down with Jilly

It was all very relaxed in Fulham. No one bothered about their gardens, and we all chucked beer cans and spare rib bones over each other's fences when we ran out of dustbin space. It was only when we moved to Putney and inherited a lovely garden which we promptly allowed to deteriorate that we discovered horticulture here was taken very seriously indeed.

Soon the street were clicking their tongues over our hayfield of a lawn, and making cracks about calling in the Forestry Commission to deal with the weeds.

Finally one kindly neighbour could bear it no longer and tactfully found us a gardener to come in three hours a week. I wasn't wild about the idea — I didn't feel our lifestyle merited anything as smart. But when he turned up glamorous and bronzed from weekends in Majorca with gold medallions and shirts slashed to the navel I soon got over my scruples.

On the first day, anxious to fortify him against the Herculean task confronting him, I made him some coffee and caught myself uttering the blushmaking phrase: 'I wonder if he takes sugar, gardeners usually do, don't they?'

And in my nervousness I unknowingly tipped two teaspoonfuls of salt into his cup. After such a dodgy start, however, we have never looked back. Every Tuesday, he arrives in a white sports car — just after my husband has left for work — which I'm sure causes more clicking than ever our weeds did. And every week, feeling extremely guilty, I draw my family allowance to pay him. He does all the boring heavy work, which leaves me free to potter round with a trowel having mini-Sissinghurst fantasies.

'Feeling a bit Vita today,' I boom to my neighbours, as I stump around snapping off dead roseheads. Any minute I shall be into tweed skirts and lisle stockings, bearing back baskets of cuttings from lunch parties, and exchanging loads of manure with my husband for Christmas.

One leads such an exciting life as a lady gardener, all the mulching and propagating and forced bedding and bastard trenching and preparing one's own fertiliser. As I rush from rose bush to rose bush, scattering hoof and horn mixture, nearly fainting from the terrible smell, I feel as though I'm taking part in some ancient fertility rite.

Immediately, too, one is drawn into a fantastic life and death struggle. Tasks for May, for example, read like an itinerary for the Borgias: 'Spray caterpillar-infested apples with lead arsenate wash, *destroy* gooseberry caterpillar with DDT, *kill* all lawn daises, fertilise roses, dried blood is safe and excellent, spray pears with arsenate wash against codlin moth.'

An even fiercer battle rages in our garden between flora and fauna. Plants don't have much hope against children and footballs, my husband having a net, fornicating tom cats, and our great flat-footed dog stampeding round smashing down peonies and lupins newly bought at 50p a throw.

My husband usually gardens on Sunday afternoon when guilt at having done nothing all weekend, coupled with hangover from lunch-time drinks, meets gloom about Monday morning head on so he's in no mood to be told he's just dug up a whole bed of dahlias.

Our garden is going through a messy stage at the moment, which also irritates him. The previous owner put in one cwt of daffodils, and we had great fun playing Wordsworth in April. But they've now reached the stage of straggling everywhere and losing their colour, a nagging reminder that after a certain age one should really have one's hair cut short.

Another bone of contention is my forgetting to turn the

sprinkler off. So we return home after a day out to find flooding and the cats perched on top of the rockery trying to bribe a nearby dove to go and look for an olive branch.

I enjoy reading gardening books, particularly the sections on topiary:

The gardener is advised to try his hand at balls before attempting bears and *peacocks*.

But, like baby books, they make everything such hard work. Not content with putting in a plant, no sooner is it doing well than you have to dig it up again and hack bits off it (euphemistically known as easing away with a handfork) and put bits back in the earth, which promptly wither and perish.

Gardening is so expensive too. Once you become a plantaholic you can't pass a gardening shop without getting out your cheque book until every available inch of plot is used up: Like a friend's husband who rushed into the kitchen clutching a half emptied seedbox wailing:

'Oh Helen, Helen, I've run out of garden.'

And there are such bizarre things to buy: 'Blended horse manure made from mushroom compost'; and last week I wavered for hours between the Hozelock Lawn Queen and the Hoselock Green Queen, I did so want to have a fairy at the bottom of my garden. Then there are kinky gardening gloves made in tan leather but with actual green thumbs.

'Repels all dirt,' says the directions. Mary Whitehouse should invest in a pair.

In fact the only person with green thumbs in our house is my housekeeper, who believes growing things respond to kindness, and spends hours a day in the conservatory chatting up the potted plants. Twice a week, she imports the entire contents into the kitchen for a soaking in water. It looks as though Birnam Wood has finally arrived from Dunsinane. Before Christmas we had an extremely tidy Au Pair, who, disliking hacking her way through the jungle, kept trying to take Birnam Wood back again. On one occasion I only just averted a collision in the kitchen doorway when I found Housekeeper and Au Pair furiously advancing on each other both completely shielded by huge

152

Sweetheart plants.

Last September my housekeeper appropriated every bowl in the house — the children had their cornflakes out of saucers for months — to grow hyacinths for Christmas. Actually they emerged with brewer's droop in time for Easter, except one tricolor arrangement, planted in a polythene box entitled Baby Teat and Bottle Sterilising Unit, which struggled out in March and was proudly placed on the drawingroom table. My husband was so delighted with this, he refused to let it be moved to some less ostentatious place.

Now summer has come, she's off growing cabbages behind the rhododendrons, and tending boxes of cucumbers like some illicit still in the potting shed.

But I'm entirely on her side. Once the gardening bug gets you, you become totally obsessed. I never believed I'd greet torrential rain with a cheer, or that when a friend came round with rivetting tidings of a new lover, my attention would be distracted by the sight of columbine tendrils curling treacherously round one of my lilies.

And there's always something to look forward to in a garden. Will the pears manage to outwit the demon codlin moth, will one Love in the Mist seedling force its way through the iron ground and survive the footballs and the ravening paws?

And nothing can beat the sheer voluptuousness of walking in your *own* garden with the cats peering out of the shrubbery like a Rousseau painting, raindrops trembling in the centre of the lupin leaves, and that marvellous mingled smell of grass mowings, wet earth, lilac, and the sun drying the dew on your *own* lavender.

Or perhaps it's just in the process of growing old that you throw away the *Kama Sutra*, and concentrate on being good in flower bed.

Carols

I love carols — they have the same shining innocence and lack of pretension as medieval frescoes. And one of my favourite pastimes is browsing and playing my way through the *Oxford Book of Carols*. From the first page one is drawn into a magic world — a sort of Monteverdi's Flying Circus — full of obscure medieval songs about cuckoos, genuflecting cherry trees, Fillpale the cow, and the Girt Dog or Langport who burnt his long tail.

Even characters as exotic as the Magi take on a cheerful homespun quality:

Three kings are here both wealthy and wise,
Come riding far o'er the snow-covered ice.
The search for the Child, the redeemer of wrong
With tambours and drums, they go sounding along.

Unlike hymn, the word carol is of a dancing origin, and meant to dance in a ring, which I suppose accounts for their joyous lilting quality:

Joseph did whistle and Mary did sing,
On Christmas Day, on Christmas Day,
And all the bells on earth did ring.

I love all the domestic touches. Mary having a pregnant woman's craving for cherries, and Joseph snapping back with understandable asperity.
'Let him pluck thee a cherry that brought thee now with child.'

I often wonder how seriously the Middle Ages took the virgin birth. They're always making sly cracks about Joseph being an old man, an old man was he.

The footnotes in the *Oxford Book* are absolute bliss. 'We regret,' writes the editor about the laxness of one parish church, 'that A Virgin Unspotted has been dropped at Grasmere.' One has visions of her coming down by parachute. And I never knew the comma in God Rest Ye Merry, Gentlemen came after the word Merry, or that Mendelssohn wrote the music for Hark the Herald Angels.

Then there are the verses of carols starred as being too secular to be sung in church:

Call up the Butler of this house
Put on his golden ring
Let him bring us a glass of beer,
And the better we shall sing.

I love the titles to the tunes: Old Winchester, Bristol, St. George, Maidstone and Sidney — they sound like cruisers or brands of sherry; and some of the authors are rather bizarre. Half the earlier carols seem to have been taken from the Latin of C. Coffin. Or written by Bishop Woodford and Compilers (which sounds more like a pop group). And typically it's only in a French carol that Mary keeps harping on about missing dinner, when poor Joseph is desperately searching for an inn.

Good King Wenceslas is wildly topical at the moment with everyone rushing round the petrol pumps gathering winter fuel. We were always ticked off at school for whooping when we sang the word 'Fu-oo-el'.

The author of Good King W, John Mason Neale (we had a good laugh over that at school) gets an absolute pasting in the *Oxford Carol Book*. The editors describe the carol as 'doggerel, poor and commonplace to the last degree, owing its popularity to the delightful tune.'

I must confess a rather soft spot for Good King W. Admittedly it does end in mid air. We never discover if the King and his deep-frozen page ever reach Yonder Peasant.

I suspect they got fed up with trailing through the snow, and drank all the wine, ate all the flesh to keep themselves warm — a sort of wassail-stop tour. History doesn't relate what they did with the pine logs.

People seem to forget there are carols for all seasons of the year, whenever there's occasion for rejoicing. I think spring and summer carols have the same exotic out-of-season glamour of autumn crocuses and Christmas roses.

John Mason Neale apart, the Victorians committed some terrible crimes in the names of carols. Mrs Alexander rabbiting on in Once in Royal David's City about tears and smiles. Christina Rossetti's fearful dirge about the bleak mid-winter: 'Snow had fallen, snow on snow, snow on snow.' She probably couldn't think what to put. She was also inaccurate. It doesn't snow in Bethlehem at Christmas. The temperature is normally around 57 degrees fahrenheit, and, says the Meteorological Office, it rains more than it does in London in December.

On the other hand, many of the twentieth-century writers recaptured the beauty and simplicity of medieval carols. Take one by Chesterton:

The Christchild stood at Mary's knee
And all his hair was like a crown
And all the flowers looked up at him
And all the stars looked down.

In the *Oxford Book*, learned doctors are always being woken at six o'clock on Christmas morning by the sweet singing of millgirls. I wish Putney carol singers would take a leaf out of their book. From mid-November we get bombarded by fat teenagers ringing our bell and to the accompaniment of stifled giggles croaking out: 'We wish you a merry Christmas,' and then forgetting the words.

I'm not very keen either on those organised parties of carol singers: a-sexual briskies; high-complexioned ladies tossing their heads in time to the music; tenors in spectacles with drips on the ends of their noses.

But then I'm always embarrassed when people sing at

me personally. Not that it stopped me carol singing as a child, hawking my Barnado's box with the hole in the bottom round the local gentry, failing miserably to reach those top Es in Hark the Herald Angels.

I'm sure people gave me money to go away.

One Christmas I was even selected to play the carols for house prayers at school. Alas, I was rather smug about it beforehand, which drove an iconoclastic friend to put Bronco inside the piano against the strings. As a result Little Town of Bethlehem came out as a sort of Honky Tonk Pizzicato. I got so flustered I missed the repeat sign in the first verse and stumbled through the whole carol two lines ahead of the choir. Fortunately our housemistress was tone-deaf.

We enjoyed carols at school. Once we started singing them, it meant the end of term was near and there were all those frightful schoolgirl jokes about shepherds washing their socks by night, and the Angel Gabriel ringing for womb service, and We Three Kings Blacking Up with Orient Tar. That Old Black Magi has me in his spell, I suppose. Today my two-year-old daughter is merrily carrying on the tradition:

Goosey, Goosey Gander
Upstairs downstairs,
In my ladies' manger.

But I think what ultimately enchants one about carols — 'those masterpieces of tantalising simplicity' — is their gaiety and grace:

The rising of the sun
The running of the deer
The playing of the merry organ

They seem to call to us from a less complex world, where people were happier, less materialistic, and delighted in making their own music together, instead of having their minds blown by a pounding of gramophones, wireless and television.

157

As the writer of the introduction to the *Oxford Book* pointed out in 1928:

'It should be possible to restore such spontaneous and imperishable things to general use . . . perhaps, nothing is just now of such importance as to increase the element of joy in religion.'

Today, he might have added the words: 'and in life' as well. Carols seem to challenge us to be merrier, love and joy come to you.

THE END

OCTAVIA
by JILLY COOPER

As soon as Octavia caught a glimpse of Jeremy in the night club, she knew she just had to have him. It didn't matter that he'd just got engaged to an old school friend of hers, plump, good natured Gussie; he was looking at Octavia in the way that suggested bed rather than breakfast, and she was weak at the knees . . . But Octavia was used to men falling in love with her at a moment's notice — it happened all the time if you were rich and as stunning as she was. An invitation to join Gussie and Jeremy for a cosy weekend on a canal barge came like a gift from the gods: How could she fail to hook Jeremy? But the other part of the foursome was whizz-kid business tycoon Gareth Llewellyn, a swarthy Welshman with all the tenderness of a scrum-half . . . definitely not Octavia's type! And one way and another, he certainly managed to thwart her plans . . .

0 552 10717 4   £1.00

A SELECTED LIST OF FINE NOVELS
THAT APPEAR IN CORGI

While every effort is made to keep prices low, it is sometimes necessary to increase prices at short notice. Corgi Books reserve the right to show new retail prices on covers which may differ from those previously advertised in the text or elsewhere.

The prices shown below were correct at the time of going to press.

☐	11525 8	**CLASS**	£1.50
☐	11149 X	**IMOGEN**	£1.00
☐	10878 2	**PRUDENCE**	£1.00
☐	10717 4	**OCTAVIA**	£1.00
☐	10576 7	**HARRIET**	£1.00
☐	10427 2	**BELLA**	£1.00
☐	10277 6	**EMILY**	£1.00
☐	11751 X	**JOLLY SUPER**	£1.25
☐	11752 8	**JOLLY SUPER TOO**	£1.25
☐	11801 X	**JOLLY SUPERLATIVE**	£1.25
☐	11802 8	**SUPER JILLY**	£1.25
☐	11832 X	**SUPER COOPER**	£1.25

ORDER FORM

All these books are available at your book shop or newsagent, or can be ordered direct from the publisher. Just tick the titles you want and fill in the form below.

CORGI BOOKS, Cash Sales Department, P.O. Box 11, Falmouth, Cornwall.

Please send cheque or postal order, no currency.

Please allow cost of book(s) plus the following for postage and packing:

U.K. Customers—Allow 40p for the first book, 18p for the second book and 13p for each additional book ordered, to a maximum charge of £1.49.

B.F.P.O. and Eire—Allow 40p for the first book, 18p for the second book plus 13p per copy for the next 3 books, thereafter 7p per book.

Overseas Customers—Allow 60p for the first book and 18p per copy for each additional book.

NAME (block letters) ....

ADDRESS ....

....